ESSENTIAL LATIN FOR LAWYERS

Russ VerSteeg

CAROLINA ACADEMIC PRESS

Durham, North Carolina

Meis Parentibus

ISBN (paperback edition) 0-89089-378-0
Library of Congress Catalog Card Number: 90-83467

Printed in the United States of America

Carolina Academic Press
700 Kent Street
Durham, North Carolina 27701
(919) 489-7486

CONTENTS

ACKNOWLEDGMENTS

I am grateful to the many people who assisted, either directly or indirectly, in the preparation of this book. I have dedicated this book to my parents, Bob and Sally, who initially encouraged me to study Latin and the Classics. I owe immeasurable gratitude to my wife, Nina, without whose patience and support I simply could not have written this book. I am also grateful to my daughter, Whitney, and my son, Carlton, who have endured many weekends without daddy as a result of my efforts to complete the manuscript. Furthermore, I must thank John W. Barclay, whose support and encouragement made my legal education possible. In addition, I am indebted to the following individuals: Dr. Christina Elliot Sorum, whose creative and inspirational teaching made the study of Latin exciting and convinced me to major in Latin; Professor Olympiad Ioffe, who supervised my initial work on this project; Lynn Daggett, Esq., Craig Tateronis, Esq., Judy Hogan, Esq., and David Cavicke, Esq., who helped me formulate and distribute my original survey for law professors at Harvard, Stanford, Yale, and the University of Connecticut; Dr. Norma Goldman, Dr. Jacob Nyenhuis, and the Wayne State University Press who have given me permission to reprint a portion of their Latin text, *Latin Via Ovid*, in the appendix; Maureen Walsh, who has provided research assistance through funding from Western New England College School of Law; the professors at the University of Connecticut, Harvard, Yale, and Stanford who took the time to complete my original survey; and my colleagues at Western New England College School of Law.

INTRODUCTION

This book is designed to assist law students, practicing attorneys, undergraduates studying Latin etymology, paralegals and students in paralegal training, and anyone else interested in the law and its Latin heritage. The vast majority of lawyers and law students today have not studied Latin. Consequently, it is natural to feel intimidated and discouraged by the inability to cope with the myriad Latin words and phrases found in legal writing. The practice of law and the study of law in law school are difficult enough in many other ways. Lawyers and law students should not be forced to contend with a Latin language barrier. Even if law students or lawyers have studied Latin in high school or in college, chances are that they no longer remember their declensions and conjugations (not to mention the peculiar legal vocabulary) well enough to fully understand the Latin legal terminology they find in their daily practice or in law school casebooks.

In this book, I translate the Latin words and phrases which lawyers, law students, and paralegals are most likely to meet.[1] Additionally, I explain the use of the Latin terminology with respect to the broader legal context in which it occurs. By both translating and explaining, I hope to help students and practitioners learn the most important and most commonly occurring Latin terms used in legal writing and to assist them in their own legal analysis and writing.[2]

I must mention that today most authorities advise students and lawyers to avoid Latin terminology in their writing whenever possible.[3] Although this advice obviously has a great deal of merit, the fact remains that modern Anglo-American law has retained thousands of Latin words, phrases, and maxims which lawyers and judges continue to use. In some instances the Latin terminology has historical value only. To be sure some use Latin in an effort to sound erudite or to intimidate adversaries.[4] But the bench and bar also utilize Latin terminology as a convenient shorthand for principles and ideas that would otherwise take paragraphs to explain. Every day lawyers and our courts prove that Latin is not a dead language.

This book is divided into two separate parts. Chapters One through Nine provide translations, discussions, and explanations of Latin legal terminology arranged according to subject matter. I have tried to isolate the most important half dozen or so Latin terms that are germane to each substantive area of law. Chapter Nine examines a handful of the most common Latin words and phrases that are found in all areas of the law. Where possible, I give concrete examples and legal authority to support the translations with a contextual framework. I think that this subject area format offers a fuller insight into the role that Latin terminology plays in the law. The second part of the book is a glossary of approximately 300 Latin terms that frequently occur in legal writing. I have tried to include only terminology that law students and lawyers are actually likely to see in study and practice. I have purposely tried to exclude truly obscure and infrequently occurring words and phrases: hence the book's title serves a genuinely descriptive purpose.

Admittedly, this book, by its very nature, covers much material which can be found in other places (e.g., a law dictionary, course outlines, etc.). However, I hope that the unique organization, arrangement, and relational format in which I present this information will prove useful for experienced practitioners, young attorneys, paralegals, and law students who encounter legal Latin.

Lastly, I have included a guide to classical Latin pronunciation in the appendix. Lawyers tend to butcher Latin pronunciation. I must admit that we have adopted anglicized pronunciations in our everyday spoken English. Nevertheless, I think that it is important to make available a reliable reference for Latin pronunciation. I hope that the legal profession can incorporate at least a semblance of proper Latin pronunciation into its daily use.

■ ENDNOTES

1. Although few would question that Anglo-American legal writing is replete with Latin terminology, because it would be difficult for any one individual to determine which Latin words and phrases are of primary importance as opposed to those which are merely ancillary, I decided to survey law professors in order to ascertain which Latin terms are the most important.

For each of the first year subjects, I asked professors to indicate which ten words/phrases they believed students would most likely encounter in their classes and would probably need to have explained. I also asked the professors not necessarily to limit their list of ten to the possibilities which I had provided on the survey. Rather, I suggested that they should feel free to add others of their own choosing (and many did just that). For the "general terms" category, I asked the professors to indicate which terms law students were most likely to meet in their course reading and which, in the opinion of the professors, any self-respecting law student should know.

I later gathered the Latin terms most commonly found in corporations/tax law and evidence to make the study more complete. My effort has been to isolate the most important half-dozen (or so) Latin terms and to discuss them in each substantive chapter.

2. In addition to translating and explaining the terms in context, as a general rule I also explain the Latin grammar of each term. I have also included a brief historical overview of the Roman law of each of the eight substantive areas entitled "The Roman Background," which I hope the reader will find interesting and worthwhile. For a more detailed treatment of ancient Roman law, let me suggest two excellent works: J. Thomas, Textbook of Roman Law (1976) and O. Ioffe, Roman Law (1987).

3. See, *e.g.*, R. Wydick, Plain English for Lawyers 53-55 (2d ed. 1985). Wydick laments that "too often lawyers use Latin . . . phrases needlessly. Sometimes they do it out of habit or haste—the old phrase is one they learned in law school, and they have never taken time to question its use. Other times they do it believing mistakenly that the old phrase's meaning cannot be expressed in ordinary English, or that the old phrase is somehow more precise than ordinary English."

4. See, *e.g.*, Getman, *Colloquy: Human Voice in Legal Discourse*, 66 Tex. L. Rev. 577 (1988), who states: "Perhaps because professional voice derives from case law of varying ages, its rhetorical style tends to be formal, erudite, and old-fashioned. Its passages often are interspersed with terms of art and Latin phrases, as though its user were removed from and slightly above the general concerns of humanity." *See also Butler v. Bruno*, 341 A. 2d 735 (1975), where Justice Kelleher of the Rhode Island Supreme Court commented:

[T]he civil-law rules are encrusted with the verbiage that is usually associated with the law of real property. When they are used, one hears such terms as easement, the dominant estate, the servient estate, and servitudes, and the classicist has the opportunity to try his hand at translating such ponderous Latin phrases as *cujus est solum, ejus usque ad coelum et ad inferos,* or *aqua currit, et debet currere ut currere solebat.*

Id. at 738.

ESSENTIAL LATIN FOR LAWYERS

CHAPTER ONE

CIVIL PROCEDURE

▌ THE ROMAN BACKGROUND

In the history of Roman jurisprudence there were basically three stages of legal procedure. The earliest of the three, the *legis actiones*, required the plaintiff to bring his defendant before a magistrate in order for the parties to make their oral declarations concerning the dispute. This process before the magistrate was called *in iure* ("in law"). Thereafter, the parties appeared before an arbitrator of their own choosing. The most striking aspect of the *legis actiones* is the relatively passive role which the state official, the magistrate, played in the process.

The *Lex Aebuta* (149-126 B.C.) established the next stage in Roman procedural development called *per formulam*, or the formulary system. Procedure *per formulam*, like the *legis actiones*, involved essentially two stages. First the plaintiff brought the defendant before the magistrate (just as he had in the *legis actiones*). However, in the *in iure* process of the formulary system the magistrate wrote down a summary of the parties' claims. He produced, in short, a blueprint for the judge who would ultimately decide the case. He instructed the judge how to go about deciding the case. In many respects, the formula which the magistrate provided for the judge was functionally similar to the instructions which a modern-day judge gives to a jury. The magistrate also appointed the judge who would hear the case on its merits. The second step in the formulary system, called *apud iudicem* ("in the presence of the judge"), was just that: the judge, appointed by the magistrate, heard the litigants' evidence and then decided the case according to the formula articulated by the magistrate. Thus, the most significant feature of procedure *per formulam* was the primary role which the magistrate played in the legal process. The third stage of ancient Roman legal procedure is the least important for students of Anglo-American law. Procedure *per cognitionem* was primarily dispute resolution through a bureaucratic imperial mechanism which provided far more administrative efficiency than justice for the parties in interest.

Our modern American rules of civil procedure govern the rules of pleading, jurisdiction, and the myriad practice technicalities by which trials and appeals move through our court system. Today the Federal Rules of Civil Procedure govern the procedural aspects of litigation in our federal courts. Each state has its own rules of court which prescribe state court practice as well.

FORUM NON CONVENIENS

A *forum non conveniens* is an "inconvenient forum," "a place of judicial business which is not suitable or appropriate."[1]

Parties can be extremely concerned about what court will decide their case and what law the court will apply. There can be any number of reasons why a litigant might prefer one court to another or the law of one jurisdiction to another. Since it is the plaintiff who initiates a lawsuit, s/he often has a choice as to where s/he brings suit. Presumably, if the plaintiff does, in fact, have a choice (i.e., if s/he is capable of obtaining jurisdiction over the defendant in more than one place), s/he probably will file suit wherever s/he believes s/he has the best chance of prevailing (i.e., wherever s/he perceives the forum to be friendliest and the law most beneficial to his/her case).

If the defendant does not like the plaintiff's choice of forum and, in fact, thinks that s/he might have a better opportunity to defend successfully in another forum, s/he typically argues either that the forum should not have jurisdiction over him/her or that, even though the forum which the plaintiff has selected does properly have jurisdiction over him/her (the defendant), that forum is impractical and/or inconvenient for one reason or another. In other words, the defendant, while admitting that s/he is subject to the forum's jurisdiction, tries to move the litigation to a different jurisdiction on the grounds of *forum non conveniens*.

However, a defendant must have persuasive reasons for wanting Forum #1 to dismiss the case in order to allow Forum #2 to take it. Simply saying, "I like Forum #2's laws better" will not do. If, for example, most of the witnesses involved in a case live in Forum #2, Forum #1 might be more willing to dismiss based on the doctrine of *forum non conveniens*. To require one person (the defendant) to travel a great distance for trial is one thing, but to ask several witnesses to do the same might be impractical or inappropriate. If Forum #2 is more familiar than Forum #1 with the state law which will apply in the case, Forum #1 might apply the doctrine of *forum non conveniens*. Also, if material evidence (i.e., not necessarily just the location of witnesses) such as important records or other documents are located in Forum #2, Forum #1 would be more inclined to dismiss on grounds of *forum non conveniens*.[2]

Piper Aircraft Co. v. Reyno[3] illustrates the doctrine of *forum non conveniens*. A small airplane manufactured by Piper crashed in Scotland killing the Scottish pilot and five Scottish passengers instantly. Reyno, the administratrix of the passengers' estates filed suit in the United States against Piper and also Hartzell Propeller, Inc., the company that manufactured the plane's propeller. Reyno also filed a separate action in the United Kingdom. The U.S. Supreme Court noted "Reyno candidly admits that the action against Piper and Hartzell was filed in the United States because its laws regarding liability, capacity to sue, and damages are more favorable to her position than are those of Scotland."[4] The Pennsylvania District Court granted Piper's motion to dismiss on grounds of *forum non conveniens*.[5]

The Third Circuit Court of Appeals reversed, primarily because Scottish law was less favorable to the plaintiff, but the U.S. Supreme Court reversed the Third Circuit and affirmed the district court's opinion.[6] The Supreme Court emphasized that all of the "real parties in interest" were Scottish citizens and all of the "[w]itnesses who could testify regarding the maintenance of the aircraft, the training of the pilot, and the investigation of the accident—all essential to the defense—are in Great Britain."[7] The Supreme Court held that merely because the substantive law applicable to a case might change, that consequence should ordinarily not be given conclusive or even substantial weight in the *forum non conveniens* inquiry.[8]

Among federal courts, 28 U.S.C. § 1404(a) provides that one federal district court may transfer a case to another federal district court on the grounds of *forum non conveniens*. This is slightly different from the application of *forum non conveniens* in most state courts where Forum #1 does not transfer the case to another court but instead dismisses it so that the case may be brought in a forum which perhaps has more practical reasons to resolve the dispute.

IN PERSONAM

This Latin phrase simply means "against the individual."[9] In order for a court's decision to be binding upon an individual (i.e., for the state to have authority to enforce the court's decision), a court must first have the authority to exercise its power over that individual. The authority to exercise its power over an individual is called "jurisdiction."[10]

Typically a forum state has jurisdiction over an individual (or a corporation) if that individual is physically present in the forum state. One of the most important cases which law students generally read in civil procedure during their first year is *Pennoyer v. Neff*.[11] In *Pennoyer* the U.S. Supreme Court, among other things, held that, if a person has been served with process in a state (i.e., a process server or sheriff has handed the legal papers directly to the individual while s/he was physically within the state's borders), that state may exercise its jurisdiction over that person.[12] In *Grace v. MacArthur*,[13] an individual was served with process while flying in an airplane over Arkansas airspace. The court held that even this limited presence in the Ozark sky was sufficient to give the federal court in the Eastern District of Arkansas jurisdiction against the person.[14]

In addition to actual, physical presence, courts have developed other theories to give forum states jurisdiction *in personam*. The most common method of obtaining *in personam* jurisdiction, other than actual physical presence, is personal jurisdiction based on domicile (that is based upon the place where a person lives and intends to stay indefinitely). Other traditional bases for *in personam* jurisdiction include consent of an individual; long-arm statutes enacted by most states, providing that any person who has committed tortious acts within that state is subject to its jurisdiction; and doing business in a state.

The most important case in the twentieth century concerning *in personam* jurisdiction is probably *International Shoe Co. v. Washington*.[15] In *International Shoe*, the U.S. Supreme Court held that, in order for a forum to assert *in personam* jurisdiction over an individual, that individual must have sufficient minimum contacts with the forum state so as not to violate the traditional notions of fair play and substantial justice.[16] This "minimum contacts" standard has also been extended to *in rem* jurisdiction in *Shaffer v. Heitner*[17] and has been considered and discussed in a long line of Supreme Court cases including *Hanson v. Denkla*,[18] *Perkins v. Benguet Consolidated Mining Co.*,[19] and *McGee v. International Life Insurance Co.*[20]

The most important case applying the *International Shoe* test for *in personam* jurisdiction is probably *World-Wide Volkswagen Corp. v. Woodson*.[21] In *World-Wide Volkswagen*, the plaintiffs bought an automobile (the car involved was actually an Audi not a Volkswagen—try that one on your friends for trivia) from World-Wide Volkswagen, a retailer in New York. The plaintiffs (a husband and wife) drove the car to Oklahoma where another vehicle crashed into the rear of the Audi, igniting a fire (allegedly caused by a defective fuel system) which severely burned the wife and her two children. Even though the court acknowledged that such an accident might be foreseeable, it held that, unless the New York retailer's "conduct and connection with the forum state are such that he should reasonably anticipate being haled into court there," Oklahoma could not properly exercise its jurisdiction over him.[22] In short, the court held that, because the retailer had "no contacts, ties, or relations with the state of Oklahoma," the state could not exercise *in personam* jurisdiction over him.[23]

International Shoe and *World-Wide Volkswagen* have established the current boundaries of *in personam* jurisdiction. These cases and the cases upon which they are based have the effect of blurring the old, traditional distinctions between *in personam*, *in rem*, and *quasi in rem* jurisdiction.[24] The importance of minimum contacts, as articulated in *International Shoe*, *McGee*, *Hanson v. Denkla*, *Shaffer*, *World-Wide Volkswagen*, and other similar cases, has, in many respects, taken over the modern-day notions of *in personam* jurisdiction (and jurisdiction in general).

IN REM

The phrase *in rem* simply means "against the thing."[25] Unlike jurisdiction *in personam*, *in rem* jurisdiction is based upon a court's authority to exercise its power over a thing, not a person. Typically, courts exercise *in rem* jurisdiction with respect to non-movable property, like real estate, or a status (generally the status of marriage). The most common type of *in rem* actions are foreclosures on real property and quiet title actions. In both foreclosure and quiet title actions, the plaintiff seeks judicial recognition of his/her rights to the title of a specific parcel of real property and judicial recognition that no one else possesses rights to the title of that same property.[26]

If you are a law student, you will discover that *in rem* jurisdiction does not occupy as prominent a position in the first-year civil procedure curriculum as *in personam* jurisdiction or as prominent a position as the hybrid, *quasi in rem* jurisdiction. *Quasi in rem* means "as if against the thing." In the days before *Shaffer v. Heitner*,[27] a plaintiff traditionally was permitted to attach (that is, have a sheriff seize in order to sell) property owned by a defendant located in the forum. The idea is actually rather simple; cagey, but simple. Suppose you live in South Carolina and I live in Florida. You paint houses for a living and I am a newspaper editor in West Palm Beach. As an investment, I buy a condo on the shore near Myrtle Beach, S.C. I never actually go to the condo myself. In fact, I have never so much as stepped foot in South Carolina in my life! Instead I rent it to beach-goers in season. I hear about what a great house painter you are and contract with you to come down to West Palm to paint my Florida home. You make the trip south and do the job. For one reason or another I am dissatisfied with the job you have done, so when I get your bill I refuse to pay you. Since you have no desire to travel to Florida and spend what may be weeks, months, or years litigating our contract dispute, you, of course, would far prefer to sue me in South Carolina and force me to come to you. It is highly doubtful that merely owning the condo in Myrtle Beach would be considered sufficient minimum contacts for you to be able to obtain *in personam* jurisdiction over me. However, under traditional notions of *quasi in rem* jurisdiction, you would be permitted to attach my condo in order to gain jurisdiction over me. Thus, even though you were incapable of getting *in personam* jurisdiction over me, and even though the condo has absolutely no relationship whatsoever to our contract dispute, you could still force me to come to South Carolina to defend the contract case, unless I wanted just to kiss the condo good-bye. If I did just that (i.e., decided not to come to South Carolina to defend) and lost the contract suit in South Carolina by default, you would then be able to get whatever money damages the court awarded for the contract from the proceeds of the sheriff's sale of my condo. The jurisdiction is called *quasi in rem* because it is "as if" you were proceeding against my property (the condo); when, in fact, you are proceeding against me (the person) on your contract claim.

Shaffer, the cases which led to *Shaffer*, and its progeny have established the general principles regarding *quasi in rem* jurisdiction. There are essentially two types of *quasi in rem* jurisdiction: *quasi in rem* type I and *quasi in rem* type II.

Type I are those cases in which the plaintiff's cause of action arises from the defendant's contacts with the forum. For example, if I had contracted with you to paint my Myrtle Beach condo (not my Florida house), then your cause of action against me would have arisen out of my contacts with the forum (i.e., my property ownership in South Carolina). In such cases (*quasi in rem* type I) it appears that even a single contact with the forum, so long as the plaintiff's cause of action actually arises from that single contact, will be enough to comply with the minimum contacts test (i.e., to not offend "traditional notions of fair play and substantial justice").[28] Thus, *quasi in rem* type I jurisdiction appears to be, at least for the present, a sound basis of jurisdiction.

Quasi in rem type II cases are those actions in which a plaintiff bases his/her cause of action upon a defendant's contact with the forum which has no relationship with the cause of action. In our original hypothetical, where you sued me in South Carolina based upon my ownership of the Myrtle Beach condo, your suit had nothing to do with my condo. Your cause of action arose from an agreement concerning Florida property, not South Carolina property. That suit was based upon *quasi in rem* type II jurisdiction. The holding in *Shaffer* essentially destroyed *quasi in rem* type II actions. However, one case which is still good law, *Perkins v. Benguet Consolidated Mining Co.*,[29] held that where the defendant's contacts with the forum are sufficiently "continuous and systematic," even if the plaintiff's cause of action does not arise from the defendant's contacts with the forum, the court may properly assert jurisdiction over the defendant.[30] Thus, it is clear that a defendant's single contact with a forum would not satisfy the minimum contacts requirements of *Shaffer* in a *quasi in rem* type II action.

Consequently, it appears that the nature and quantity of contacts which a defendant has with a potential forum are critically important in resolving the question of whether that forum can exercise *quasi in rem* jurisdiction over him/her. If those contacts are "systematic and continuous" the forum can probably exercise jurisdiction based upon either *quasi in rem* type I or *quasi in rem* type II. If the defendant has had only a single contact with the forum, although the forum might be able to assert *quasi in rem* type I jurisdiction over a defendant, relying on *McGee* (and even this reliance is questionable today), in light of *Shaffer*, it is clear that it could not exercise *quasi in rem* type II jurisdiction.

Although law students study *in personam*, *in rem*, and *quasi in rem* jurisdiction in civil procedure, it is useful to remember that *International Shoe*, *Shaffer*, and their progeny have rendered the distinctions between these almost meaningless. The crucial question in issues of jurisdiction today is whether the defendant has sufficient minimum contacts with the forum so that the forum's exercise of jurisdiction does not offend "traditional notions of fair play and substantial justice."

RES JUDICATA

The phrase *res judicata* means "a thing which has been decided."[31] It makes good common sense that, if one competent court takes the time and effort (and undergoes the expense) of deciding a particular matter, we ought not allow another court to bother attempting to resolve that same matter a second time. To do so would be a waste of judicial resources. Of course this is not to say that we ought not have an appeals process; that does make sense to correct judicial error. However, it would make no sense, for example, to allow a plaintiff who has lost a contract suit in New Jersey, to file the suit again in New York, hoping for a more favorable result on the second go-round. How would we know which court's decision to follow? Therefore, if the plaintiff is not pleased with the New Jersey result, s/he should file an appeal with the appropriate court of appeals.

But how do we know when an issue has been decided? How can we be certain that an issue should be considered *res judicata*? One of the clearest discussions of *res judicata* appears in *Blonder-Tongue Laboratories, Inc. v. University of Illinois Foundation.*[32] *Blonder-Tongue* is a patent case in which the patent at issue was for a specific type of color television antenna. To make a long story short, the court held that if one court were to adjudge a patent invalid, a subsequent court would be bound to recognize the judgment of invalidity by the first court if: (1) the patentee/licensor had received a final judgment on the merits of the patent; (2) the issue decided in the first adjudication was the same as that at issue in the subsequent case; and (3) the party against whom the plea of *res judicata* is being asserted is the same as in the first litigation or in privity with that party.[33] Justice White's opinion quoted Justice Traynor (of the California Supreme Court) in *Bernhard v. Bank of America National Trust & Savings Association,*[34] who said:

> In determining the validity of a plea of res judicata three questions are pertinent: Was the issue decided in the prior adjudication identical with the one presented in the action in question? Was there a final judgment on the merits? Was the party against whom the plea is asserted a party or in privity with a party to the prior adjudication?[35]

Justice White's decision in *Blonder-Tongue* mirrors the questions asked by Justice Traynor in *Bernhard v. Bank of America.* These, then, are the questions which lawyers and law students must ask themselves whenever the issue of *res judicata* arises (either in a case for a practicing attorney or on an exam for the student). These are the questions which must be answered in order to determine whether an issue has been sufficiently resolved so that another court can say that "the thing has been decided." If a court determines that an issue is, in fact, *res judicata*, the party attempting to relitigate the issue will be unsuccessful.[36]

SUBPOENA DUCES TECUM

Most people have some idea of what a subpoena is. The word *subpoena* is actually a combination of two Latin words: *sub* ("under") + *poena* ("penalty"). The most common use of a subpoena is the process whereby a marshal, deputy, or similar official gives a legal document to a person which commands that "person to whom it is directed to attend and give testimony at a time and place therein specified."[37] If the person to whom the subpoena is directed fails to appear, s/he is "under penalty" of law. In other words, a subpoena is materially different from a summons (which merely requests a person's presence) because it (a subpoena) provides sanctions (penalties) if a person fails to comply. Federal Rule of Civil Procedure 45(f), "Contempt," provides that, "Failure by any person without adequate excuse to obey a subpoena served upon him may be deemed a contempt of the court from which the subpoena issued."

The entire phrase, *subpoena duces tecum* means "under penalty, you will bring with you."[38]

Unlike the most common type of subpoena which merely directs a witness to appear to testify, a *subpoena duces tecum* "command[s] the person to whom it is directed to produce . . . books, papers, documents, or tangible things."[39]

In *Donovan v. Lone Steer, Inc.*,[40] a case brought by the U.S. Secretary of Labor against a restaurant-motel, the U.S. Supreme Court held that a *subpoena duces tecum* that merely directed the restaurant-motel to produce certain wage and hour records was not prohibited and did not violate the fourth amendment.[41]

STARE DECISIS

The phrase *stare decisis* means "to stand firmly by those things which have been decided."[42]

Stare decisis is the principle upon which the common law in England and America is based. Early in their law school careers, law students learn that American law today has essentially two components. Various rule-making bodies, like legislatures and other regulatory agencies such as the Environmental Protection Agency, produce "laws" which we call statutes, or regulations. In addition to statutes and regulations, courts also create laws. Courts create law by applying jurisprudential principles which have developed over centuries. They also make law by interpreting statutes and regulations.

The doctrine of *stare decisis* insists that we have consistency in our legal system. Part of our sense of fairness and justice dictates that persons similarly situated ought to be treated similarly.

A great deal of what lawyers do is to try to find judicial precedent. When a client comes into the office with a problem, the world being what it is, chances are that other people at some time have had similar problems, similar disputes. The lawyer's job, at least in part, is to try to find cases in which the parties have had disputes similar to the dispute that their client presently has. What lawyers are looking for are cases whose relevant facts are the same as, or similar to, their client's. Once the attorney has found that case or those cases, the task has just begun.[43]

As an example, let's assume that you represent a client who was injured when another driver struck his car manufactured by the A,B,C Auto Corp. in the rear and the car's gas tank exploded. Let's look at the first case you found, we'll call it *Smith v. A,B,C Corp.* In *Smith v. A,B,C Corp.* the circumstances of the parties involved and the issues presented to the court are substantially similar to those which are involved in your client's case. In addition, the court in *Smith v. A,B,C Corp.* decided in favor of your client's position. You like this case because, now, you can explain this case to your judge and argue that, based upon *stare decisis*, the universal legal principle that tells us that we ought "to stand firmly by those things which have been decided," your client should win. "Judge," you say, "in *Smith v. A,B,C Corp.*, Smith and A,B,C Corp. were arguing about negligence in a rear-end collision. Your Honor, from the facts before you, you can see that my client and the defendant in this case are also arguing about negligence in a rear end collision and all of the relevant facts in the instant case are analogous to those in *Smith v. A,B,C Corp.* Therefore, since the judge in *Smith v. A,B,C Corp.* determined that Smith (who was in exactly the same position as my client) should prevail, you, too, should follow that same judicial wisdom and also decide that my client should win." Of course there are always some facts in your client's case that are slightly different from those in the case which you are offering as precedent. Your job, then, is to convince the judge that those facts which are different are irrelevant or otherwise insignificant. "Yes, your Honor, there are some things about *Smith v. A,B,C Corp.* which are different from my client's case; but the fact that the '78 A,B,C sedan whose gas tank exploded in that case was green and my client's '78 A,B,C sedan was red is irrelevant to the question of liability."

Now let's look at the next relevant case you find, we'll call it *Jones v. A,B,C Corp. Jones v. A,B,C Corp.*, like *Smith v. A,B,C Corp.*, has facts which are very similar to your client's situation. However, in *Jones v. A,B,C Corp.*, the court decided in favor of the defendant. Now you have your work cut out for you. You must find some facts which distinguish *Jones v. A,B,C Corp.* from your client's case. If you cannot, the defendant will, no doubt, use *Jones v. A,B,C Corp.* against you, just like you will try to use *Smith v. A,B,C Corp.* against him. "Yes, your Honor, I know that the plaintiff in *Jones v. A,B,C Corp.* was also driving a '78 A,B,C sedan when it exploded and the court in that case did not find the A,B,C Corp. liable. But in *Jones v. A,B,C Corp.*, the plaintiff was transporting gasoline in the trunk when his car exploded; my client was not." That is the type of fact lawyers look for when a case appears similar to their facts but the decision goes against them: facts which are distinguishable in a relevant way.

The relative power of the courts involved in the decisions is important also. If you are arguing in a trial court, the precedents from the state's appellate court are more influential than that of another trial court. Similarly, decisions from the state's highest court, usually called the supreme court, will be binding upon the trial court (i.e., the trial court is compelled to follow decisions from the state's highest court).

As you can see, the Anglo-American tradition of *stare decisis* is infinitely important. To be sure, the doctrine of *stare decisis* does not arm a party with an impenetrable shield. Courts do not blindly follow precedent for the mere sake of following precedent. There can be sensible and logical reasons for discarding *stare decisis* when to follow it would be out of step with modern notions of reason and justice. Sometimes our society has changed in such significant ways from the time when one case was decided to the next that a court will overrule an earlier decision. Sometimes the public policy which was the underpinning of an earlier decision will no longer be compelling.[44] However, before you argue that a court ought not stand firmly by its earlier decisions, be certain that you have sound and cogent reasons for asking the judge to dispense with the general policy of *stare decisis*.

■ ENDNOTES

1. The Latin word *forum* originally meant simply "an open square" or "market-place." In time it came to mean any place of public business, such as commercial, political, or judicial business. *Conveniens* is the present active participle of the verb *convenire* ("to come together, to assemble") meaning literally "assembling." *Non* simply means "not." Literally, then, *forum non conveniens*, in the modern legal context, means "a place of judicial business not [for] assembling." Of course, the English word "convenient" ("suitable, appropriate") also comes from *conveniens*. This more recent shade of meaning for the word *conveniens* is probably more helpful in understanding the Latin phrase *forum non conveniens* in Anglo-American law today.

2. *See generally Gulf Oil Corp. v. Gilbert,* 330 U.S. 501 (1947).

3. 454 U.S. 235 (1982).

4. *Id.* at 240.

5. *Id.* at 241.

6. *Id.* at 244-60.

7. *Id.* at 242.

8. *Id.* at 249-50.

9. The preposition *in* can have a number of meanings. Here it means "against." *Personam* is the accusative singular of the noun, *persona*, which means "mask," "role," or "individuality."

10. The word "jurisdiction" itself comes from the Latin words *jus*, "law," and *dicere*, "to speak"; thus, jurisdiction is the authority to pronounce what the law in a particular area will be.

11. 95 U.S. 714 (1877).

12. *Id.* at 734.

13. 170 F. Supp. 442 (E.D. Ark. 1959).

14. *Id.* at 447.

15. 326 U.S. 310 (1945).

16. *Id.* at 320.

17. 433 U.S. 186 (1977). For more about *in rem* jurisdiction, *see In Rem, infra.*

18. 357 U.S. 235 (1952).

19. 342 U.S. 437 (1952).

20. 355 U.S. 220 (1957).

21. 444 U.S. 286 (1980).

22. *Id.* at 297.

23. *Id.* at 299.

24. *See In Rem, infra,* for more about *in rem* and *quasi in rem* jurisdiction. Also note that the U.S. Supreme Court continues to interpret these principles in light of unique fact patterns. *See, e.g., Burger King Corp. v. Rudzewicz,* 471 U.S. 462 (1985); *Keeton v. Hustler Magazine, Inc.,* 465

U.S. 770 (1984); *Helicopteros Nacionales de Colombia v. Hall*, 466 U.S. 408 (1984); *Calder v. Jones*, 465 U.S. 783 (1984).

25. Here, the preposition *in*, taking the accusative, means "against." *Rem* is the accusative singular of *res* (thing).

26. Take note, however, that some scholars may classify actions like quiet title and foreclosure as "*quasi in rem* type I" (*see* discussion of *quasi in rem*, *infra*) and argue that the only pure *in rem* actions are those involving probate, bankruptcy, escheat, or divorce.

27. *See In Personam, supra*.

28. *See McGee v. International Life Insurance Co.*, 355 U.S. 220, 223 (1957).

29. 342 U.S. 437 (1952).

30. *Id*. at 448.

31. The Latin word *res* means "thing." The word *judicata* is a perfect passive participle from the verb *judicare* ("to judge" or "to decide"), and, thus, means literally "having been decided."

32. 402 U.S. 313 (1971).

33. *Id*. at 323-24.

34. 19 Cal. 2d 807, 122 P.2d 892 (1942).

35. *Id*. at 813, 122 P.2d at 895.

36. Although a law student's study of *res judicata* will probably introduce terms like "claim preclusion," "issue preclusion," "merger," "bar," and "full faith and credit," the key issues to be resolved are reflected in Justice Traynor's three questions.

37. *See* Fed. R. Civ. P. 45(a).

38. *Duces* is the second-person singular active future tense of the Latin verb *ducere* ("to draw along, to lead"). As such, *duces* means "you will lead" or "you will bring." *Tecum* is a combination of two Latin words: *cum* (a preposition meaning "with") and *te* (the ablative singular form of the pronoun *tu* meaning "you"). The combination, *tecum*, is a Latin construction called an ablative of accompaniment.

39. Fed. R. Civ. P. 45(b).

40. 464 U.S. 508 (1984).

41. *Id*.

42. *Stare* is the present active infinitive of the Latin verb *stare* and means "to stand firm, to stand fast by." *Decisis* is an ablative plural form of the perfect passive participle of the verb *decidere*. *Decidere* is most commonly used to mean "to cut down" or "to cut off." However, it can also mean, and in this particular legal context unquestionably means, "to bring to a conclusion, settle, decide."

43. A discussion of how to find the cases through legal research is well beyond the scope of this book. One particularly good book on this subject is R. Wren and J. Wren, The Legal Research Manual (2d ed. 1986).

44. In *Helvering v. Hallock*, 309 U.S. 106, 119 (1940), Justice Frankfurter explained that "*stare decisis* is a principle of policy and not a mechanical

formula of adherence to the latest decision however recent and questionable, when such adherence involves collision with a prior doctrine more embracing in its scope, intrinsically sounder, and verified by experience." Justice Thurgood Marshall has described *stare decisis* as

> the means by which we ensure that the law will not merely change erratically, but will develop in a principled and intelligible fashion. That doctrine permits society to presume that bedrock principles are founded in the law rather than in the proclivities of individuals, and thereby contributes to the integrity of our constitutional system of government, both in appearance and in fact. While *stare decisis* is not an inexorable command, the careful observer will discern that any detours from the straight path of *stare decisis* in our past have occurred for articulable reasons, and only when the Court has felt obliged 'to bring its opinions into agreement with experience and with facts newly ascertained.' *Burnet v. Coronado Oil & Gas Co.,* 285 U.S. 383, 412 (1932) (Brandeis, J., dissenting). Our history does not impose any rigid formula to constrain the Court in the disposition of cases. Rather, its lesson is that every successful proponent of overruling precedent has borne the heavy burden of persuading the Court that changes in society or in the law dictate that the values served by *stare decisis* yield in favor of a greater objective.

Vasquez v. Hillery, 474 U.S. 254, 265-66 (1985).

CHAPTER TWO

CONSTITUTIONAL LAW

■ THE ROMAN BACKGROUND

The Romans of Cicero's day did not really have a constitution comparable to the U.S. Constitution. The legal document which the Romans revered as much as we revere our United States Constitution was probably the Laws of the Twelve Tables. The Twelve Tables, drafted about 450 B.C., represent the first codified, written laws in the ancient Roman world. It was from the Twelve Tables that the Romans derived a great many of the fundamental principles which influenced their laws throughout Roman history. According to Cicero, Roman schoolboys learned them by heart.

Nevertheless, by the time of Justinian (c. 533 A.D.), the old Latin word, *constitutio*, had acquired greater significance. In fact, Justinian's Code was comprised of hundreds of *novellae constitutiones*, "new principles."

United States constitutional law today is the body of law that has evolved as a result of court decisions interpreting the U.S. Constitution. Lawyers often confront problems related to key constitutional principles such as due process, the commerce clause, federalism, eminent domain, separation of powers, and the individual freedoms articulated in the Bill of Rights.

AMICUS CURIAE

The term *amicus curiae* means "a friend of the court."[1]

In important cases, where the outcome will likely affect a great number of people in a particular group, a court often permits that

19

group or a representative of it to file an *amicus curiae* brief. It makes good common sense to allow a group which has a significant stake in the determination of a particular issue to express its views on that issue. For example, groups such as the A.C.L.U. and the N.A.A.C.P. are likely to file *amicus curiae* briefs is in federal civil rights cases; Friends of the Earth and the Sierra Club are groups which would be likely to file *amicus curiae* briefs in environmental cases. The United States government probably files more *amicus curiae* briefs than any other single entity (the government has a stake in a relatively high percentage of federal cases). An individual may also file an *amicus curiae* brief, although an individual is much less likely to do so than a public interest group or the government. *Amicus curiae* briefs are particularly important in cases which law students read in constitutional law. By their very nature constitutional cases generally deal with some of the most important issues and rights in the legal spectrum. Thus, a broad range of groups are capable of having a keen interest in the determination of any given constitutional case, and hence, may want to file an *amicus curiae* brief in order to argue for the outcome which they deem most beneficial to their particular group.[2]

CERTIORARI

Certiorari literally means "to be informed" or "to be apprised."[3]

There are only two routes to the Supreme Court: appeal or a grant of *certiorari*. Federal law provides that, if the highest court in any one of the United States has upheld a state statute which had been challenged as violative of the Constitution or federal law, or if that court has held that a federal treaty or statute is invalid, the U.S. Supreme Court is required to hear the cases so ruling, by right of appeal.[4] Federal statute also provides that, if a federal court of appeals has held a state statute unconstitutional, the U.S. Supreme Court is also required to hear that case on appeal.[5]

For all other cases decided in state or federal courts, in order to have a case heard by the U.S. Supreme Court, the party seeking the review of the Supreme Court must apply for *certiorari*. Although the grant of *certiorari* is completely discretionary, the Supreme Court generally only grants *certiorari* when the Justices believe that some clarification is necessary. This usually occurs when one federal appeals court has reached a different conclusion from another federal appeals court in cases involving the same or nearly the same issue, when the same type of conflict arises between two or more of the highest courts in the states, or when the U.S. Supreme Court determines that it is necessary to express its view on some significant federal issue. Before the Supreme Court will grant *certiorari*, four Justices must agree that the case is important enough to warrant review.

Thus, the Latin translation, "to be made more certain," or "to be apprised" makes sense. The Supreme Court grants *certiorari* when an issue is important enough that the nation be made more certain, informed, or apprised of what the definitive law will be on a particular issue.

DE FACTO & DE JURE

De facto literally means "from that which has been done."[6] *De jure* literally means "from the law."[7] Generally, if something is done *de facto*, it is done inadvertently, without any conscious plan to bring about the result. If, on the other hand, something is done *de jure*, it is done through a purposeful, planned process.

The terms *de facto* and *de jure* are particularly important in constitutional law in a number of contexts and especially in the context of racial segregation. The early Supreme Court cases involving racial segregation addressed segregation which was characterized as *de jure* because legislators or school boards had consciously decided to segregate the schools. In *Keyes v. School District #1*,[8] the U.S. Supreme Court was faced with a problem of *de facto* segregation. In Denver (where School District #1 was located) the segregation of whites from blacks and Hispanics was certainly not the result of legislation and apparently not the result of any conscious effort to segregate. The Supreme Court held that a federal court could not order desegregation where the segregation at issue was merely *de facto* and not *de jure*. In his concurrence, Justice Powell advocated abandoning the distinction between the way that the Court viewed *de facto* as opposed to *de jure* segregation. Subsequent cases have not significantly altered the *de facto/de jure* distinction articulated in *Keyes*.[9]

INTER[STATE] & INTRA[STATE]

The English language uses *inter* and *intra* as prefixes. In Latin they are primarily prepositions. *Inter* means "between" or "among." *Intra* means "within." Thus, if you take an interstate trip, by definition, you must travel between or among two or more states. On the other hand, if you take an intrastate trip, by definition, you only travel within one state.

The U.S. Constitution grants Congress the power "to regulate commerce . . . among the several states."[10] This is the Commerce Clause of the Constitution.[11] It is important to recognize that the Commerce Clause explicitly grants Congress the authority to legislate regarding all matters dealing with interstate commerce (that is "commerce . . . among the several states"). It logically follows from the Latin maxim, *expressio unius est exclusio alterius* ("the expression of one thing is the exclusion of another") that any commerce which is entirely intrastate is left to the states to regulate within their own borders.

The "Granddaddy" of all Commerce Clause cases is *Gibbons v. Ogden*.[12] In *Gibbons*, Chief Justice John Marshall articulated an expansive view of the Commerce Clause holding that the word "commerce" includes a broad range of activity.[13] Subsequent cases involving the Commerce Clause have expanded the interpretation of what "commerce" is to the point that the Commerce Clause arguably affects just about every activity imaginable.[14]

MANDAMUS

Mandamus literally means "we command" or "we order."[15] Within the context of constitutional law, the word *mandamus* almost always refers to "a writ of *mandamus*." Generally speaking, a party seeks a writ of *mandamus* when s/he believes that someone (usually a judge or administrative official) has abused his/her power by failing to perform some ministerial duty which s/he is legally bound to perform.[16]

Thus, when a party believes that either a district court or a U.S. court of appeals has failed to perform a duty which is arguably ministerial, that party may ask the U.S. Supreme Court for a writ of *mandamus* to compel the lower federal court to perform that ministerial duty.

Marbury v. Madison[17] came to the Supreme Court on a writ of *mandamus.* Just prior to leaving office, President John Adams appointed William Marbury as a justice of the peace (he also appointed a number of other justices of the peace and judges too). Adams signed the papers but they were not delivered before he left the presidency. When Thomas Jefferson became President, his Secretary of State, James Madison, refused to deliver Marbury's commission (and the other commissions as well). Marbury argued that Madison had no discretion in the matter (i.e., that delivery of the commissions was a purely ministerial duty). Thus, Marbury was asking the Supreme Court to say, in effect, "Mr. Madison, we command you to deliver that commission to Mr. Marbury." In perhaps the most celebrated opinion in Constitutional history, Chief Justice Marshall ultimately decided that § 13 of the Judiciary Act of 1789, which Marshall interpreted as granting original jurisdiction to the Supreme Court "to issue writs of mandamus, in cases warranted by the principles and usages of law, to any courts appointed, or persons holding office, under the authority of the United States," was unconstitutional because it conflicted with article III, § 2 of the Constitution.[18]

PENUMBRA

The word *penumbra* means "a partial shadow."[19] This admittedly vague notion holds center stage in the famous Supreme Court case, *Griswold v. Connecticut.*[20] Connecticut authorities arrested Griswold, who was the executive director of the Planned Parenthood League of Connecticut, and a Yale medical professor, pursuant to a Connecticut statute which prohibited the use of "any drug, medicinal article or instrument for the purpose of preventing conception." The Supreme Court (Justice Douglas writing the divided opinion) held that the first amendment's guarantees of freedom of religion, speech, the press, assembly, and the right "to Petition the Government for a redress of grievances" extend to cast "a penumbra where privacy is protected from governmental intrusion."[21] Douglas furthermore stated that the "specific guarantees in the Bill of Rights have penumbras, formed by emanations from those guarantees that help give them life and substance."[22] In short, then, the Bill of Rights casts "somewhat of a shadow" where privacy is concerned to the extent that the whole is greater than the sum of the parts (so to speak).

Thus, the Supreme Court held that the Connecticut statute was unconstitutional because it purported to cast light on the penumbra which protects the privacy created by the Bill of Rights.[23]

■ ENDNOTES

1. The noun *amicus* simply means "friend." The place where the Roman senate met was called the *Curia*. In time the word *curia* also came to mean the senate itself. In the phrase *amicus curiae*, the word *curia* has come to mean "a decision-making body," in particular, "a court."

2. *See*, e.g., *Roe v. Wade*, 410 U.S. 113 (1973), the famous U.S. Supreme Court decision involving abortion rights, where thirty-six pro-abortion organizations and eleven anti-abortion organizations filed *amicus curiae* briefs.

3. The word *certiorari* originates from the Latin adjective *certus*, which means "fixed, certain, sure." *Certior* is the comparative form of *certus* and thus means "more certain." From *certior* came the Latin idiom *certiorem facere*, "to make more certain" (i.e., "to inform"). Later still, the Romans developed a shortened version of *certiorem facere*, the single verb *certioro*, "I inform." This verb, *certioro*, occurs only in legal contexts and is used most frequently by Ulpian and Gaius (two of the most prolific sources for Roman law). The form which has become fixed in Anglo-American legal terminology, *certiorari*, is the passive infinitive of *certioro*.

4. 28 U.S.C. §1257 (1982).

5. 28 U.S.C. §1254 (1982).

6. The preposition *de* here means "from" and *facto* is the ablative singular of the perfect passive participle of the verb *facere* ("to make" or "to do").

7. The preposition *de* again here means "from" and *jure* is the ablative singular of the noun *jus* ("law").

8. 413 U.S. 189 (1973).

9. *See*, e.g., *Milliken v. Bradley*, 418 U.S. 717 (1974); *Columbus Bd. of Educ. v. Penick*, 443 U.S. 449 (1979); and *Dayton Bd. of Educ. v. Brinkman*, 443 U.S. 526 (1979).

10. U.S. Const. art. I, § 8 cl. 3.

11. There is absolutely no way that a law student can take a constitutional law class in an American law school and not spend what will probably seem like an interminable number of class hours discussing the Commerce Clause.

12. 9 Wheat. 1 (1824).

13. *Id.* at 193-194.

14. *See*, e.g., *Katzenbach v. McClung*, 379 U.S. 294 (1964). (Where the court held that Ollie's Barbecue, a restaurant in Birmingham, Alabama, was

involved in interstate commerce because some 40% of its food was bought from out of state, even though Ollie's was not close to any interstate highway or mass transportation and apparently had a negligible number of interstate travelers as patrons.)

15. The word *mandamus* is the first-person plural present tense, active form of the Latin verb *mandare* ("to order" or "to command"). In classical Latin, when *mandare* was used in this sense, it was generally followed by a subjunctive construction in which someone was ordered to perform a certain task or to do a specific thing.

16. A ministerial duty is one which requires no discretion on the part of the individual who is supposed to perform that duty.

17. 1 Cranch 137 (1803).

18. *Id.* at 173, 176, 178.

19. The word *penumbra* is actually an anglicized combination of two Latin words: *paene*, meaning "almost," and *umbra*, meaning "shade" or "shadow."

20. 381 U.S. 479 (1965).

21. *Id.* at 483.

22. *Id.* at 484.

23. *Id.* at 485. Don't feel badly if you have a hard time swallowing Justice Douglas's "penumbra doctrine." Justice Stewart's dissent, Justice Black's dissent, and a host of subsequent legal commentators have criticized the *penumbra*, or "partial shadow," theory of the Bill of Rights.

CHAPTER THREE

CONTRACTS

■ THE ROMAN BACKGROUND

Interestingly enough, the very word "contract" comes from the Latin verb *contrahere*, "to drag, pull, lead together." Thus, the participial form, *contractus*, means "having been dragged, pulled, led together."

In ancient Roman law, the law of contracts was part of the more general law of obligations. In his book, *Ancient Law*, Sir Henry Sumner Maine used the development of contract law in ancient Rome to illustrate his thesis that, in progressive societies, a person's ability to conduct business gradually becomes more dependent on an increasing ability to change his/her position in life by contracting, rather than dependent upon his/her status. The earliest form of contract in ancient Rome was called *stipulatio*. *Stipulatio* was a method of contracting which required the parties to recite a rigid formulaic question-and-answer: "Do you promise to pay me A, B, and C?" "Yes, I promise to pay you A, B, and C." The next type of contract which evolved in Roman jurisprudence was called a "literal" contract. The Roman head of the household kept a ledger book of money owed. By writing a debt down in the ledger, a contract was deemed to have been created. The Romans next developed a group of contracts dealing with the delivery of certain types of things. These contracts were called "real" contracts ("real" is derived from the Latin word for "thing," *res*). There were essentially four types of real contracts. One involved a loan of fungible goods (*mutum*); another the loan of a specific thing (*commodatum*); still another dealt with the delivery of a movable thing for the benefit of the deliveror (*depositum*); and yet another created a type of creditor/debtor relationship (*pignus*). Finally, Roman law progressed to the point where all that was required to create a contract was the simple agreement of the parties. These contracts were called "consensual" contracts. There were four basic types of consensual contracts which evolved. *Emptio Venditio* was a contract involving sale and purchase in which all that was necessary was for the buyer and seller to agree on a price and the subject matter of the contract (i.e., they both had to agree about just what it was that one was selling and the other buying). *Locatio Conductio* was a type of contract by which several types of letting and hiring occurred. The Roman contract of *societas* created a partnership. And *mandatum* was a contract whereby one party promised gratuitous service for another (of course, such a contract would be unenforceable under the Anglo-American principles of contract law which require consideration). So it is true that Roman contract law progressively advanced from very formal, formulaic requirements for creating a contract to a stage at which parties merely had to agree, without a strictly delineated pattern or structure (such as the *stipulatio* or literal contract).

Modern contract law deals with the manner in which parties reach enforceable agreements. Law students typically study concepts such as offer and acceptance, consideration, conditions, contract remedies, and others. Law professors generally also cover areas related to contract law such as restitution, unjust enrichment, and quasi-contracts.

AB INITIO

The Latin phrase *ab initio* simply means "from the beginning."[1] Most of the cases which law students study in contracts involve situations in which two parties have made a contract and then something has gone wrong.[2] However, the agreement process itself is important because if there is no contract formed to begin with, it is impossible for a party to breach. How can someone breach a contract that was never made? Thus, when analyzing contract problems, both in practice and in law school, it is crucial to look carefully at the circumstances *ab initio*; that is, at the circumstances from the very beginning of the contracting process.

One of the reasons why the circumstances *ab initio* are so important is the issue of damages. In general, a plaintiff who alleges that a defendant has breached a contract is asking the court to order that defendant either to do exactly what s/he (the defendant) promised to do under the terms of their agreement[3] or to pay an amount of money equal to that which the plaintiff would have realized had the defendant not breached.[4] However, if for whatever reason, the contract was void or unenforceable *ab initio*, the plaintiff generally cannot recover expectation damages but will have to accept something less.[5] Contracts professors ordinarily discuss many reasons why a contract might be void or unenforceable *ab initio*. Some of the more common reasons why a "contract" might be no good from the start are the following:

(1) Lack of Consideration:

Law students inevitably spend many hours agonizing over the concept of consideration. In order to have a valid contract under American law, there must be consideration. In order to have consideration, the parties must exchange one thing for another.[6] In most contracts, parties exchange promises regarding some future activity. I promise to pay you $10 and you promise to shovel my driveway. We usually frame the promises in a conditional statement like "I promise to pay you $10 if you promise to shovel my driveway." However, if an agreement lacks consideration, it is void *ab initio*.

(2) Absence of a Valid Offer or Acceptance:

Contracts require a valid offer and an acceptance of that offer. Without both offer and acceptance, it is void *ab initio*. If I say, "I'll pay you $10 if you shovel my driveway" and you answer "OK" or better yet, "OK, I'll shovel your driveway for $10," we have a contract; there has been a valid offer and acceptance. On the other hand, if you instead answer, "I'll do it for $15," we don't have a contract. What your statement has actually done is create a counteroffer. If I answered you by saying, "OK, I'll pay you $15," we again would have a good contract, this time because I accepted your counteroffer. If there is no valid offer and acceptance, for example, if after you answered, "I'll do it for $15," I had not said anything further but merely walked away, and if you had then gone ahead and shoveled my driveway anyway, you could not, then, have recovered $15 from me, because, *ab initio*, there was no valid offer and acceptance and therefore no valid contract.

(3) Mistake:

Contracts can also be void *ab initio* due to mistake. For example, if I offered to sell you my bureau for $500 and you, thinking I had said "my Van Gogh," had accepted my offer, the "contract" would be invalid because we were mistaken concerning the subject matter of our agreement. Thus, in a very real sense, we never really agreed because the "contract" was worthless *ab initio*.

(4) Incapacity:

In our society the law presumes that certain persons are incapable of entering into legally binding agreements. Minors and persons who have been adjudged mental incompetents are the most common examples. Such persons lack the capacity to contract. Thus, any agreement with a person whom the law deems incapable of contracting is, *ab initio*, unenforceable against that person. However, the person who lacks capacity may enforce the agreement against the other party. An agreement between a minor and an adult is said to be "voidable" by the minor. The power to avoid the contract is something which a minor or other person who lacks capacity has from the inception of the agreement, *ab initio*.

(5) Duress:

A classic example of duress would be a situation where one party holds a revolver to the head of the other, threatening to shoot unless the threatened party signs the contract. Such coercion renders the "contract" void from the beginning.[7]

(6) Misrepresentation:

If I offer to sell you my color television set, telling you that it gets great reception (knowing all along that the set is really black and white and really has a blown tube to boot), that contract is voidable at the outset due to my misrepresentation. In addition to any express warranties which a seller may make, the law imposes a number of implied warranties as well. The Uniform Commercial Code [hereinafter "UCC"] § 2-314 imposes an implied warranty of merchantability that goods must be "fit for the ordinary purposes for which such goods are used." Thus, a "contract" for goods which are not so fit is voidable by the purchaser *ab initio.*

(7) Public Policy:

The law makes contracts for certain types of goods and services unenforceable due to matters of public policy (and public policy often turns on legality). For example, courts will not enforce a "contract" for the sale of cocaine, sex, or a counterfeiting machine. Contracts concerning these goods and services, and many others like them, are unenforceable because they violate public policy. In fact, they too are unenforceable *ab initio* by their very nature.[8]

ALEA[TORY] PROMISE/CONTRACT

The English adjective "aleatory" comes from the Latin noun, *alea,* meaning "a game with dice, a game of hazard" or "chance." In time the word also came to mean anything uncertain or contingent: "an accident, chance, hazard, venture, risk."[9]

The Restatement (Second) of Contracts § 379 comment (a) defines an aleatory contract as "one in which at least one party is under a duty that is conditional on the occurrence of an event that, so far as the parties to the contract are aware, is dependent on chance. Its occurrence may be within the control of third persons or beyond the control of any person." The most common type of aleatory contract (albeit generally illegal and unenforceable) is a gambling or betting contract.

The most common type of legal aleatory contract is an insurance contract under the terms of which one party, the insurer, promises to pay a large sum of money if a certain event occurs (e.g, death, theft, flood, fire, etc.) in return for the other party's (the insured's) promise to pay premiums.

Aleatory contracts are especially relevant to contract conditions and questions concerning breach of contract.

Several types of conditions affect contracts (conditions precedent and conditions subsequent being the most important). However, it is easy to see that aleatory contracts, by definition, always involve a condition. The conditions in aleatory contracts are always conditions precedent. In other words, performance by one party is contingent or conditioned on the occurrence of some event (which, in the case of aleatory contracts, is beyond the control of the parties). Only when that event takes place is one of the parties required to perform. For example, in the case of an insurance contract, a fire destroying a home can be a condition precedent to the insurance company paying the insured.[10]

There are special rules which govern what constitutes the breach of an aleatory contract. If an insured party fails to pay his/her premium, before the insurer can legally treat the insured's failure to pay as a material breach of the contract, s/he (the insurer) must first notify the insured of his/her intention to do so.[11]

ASSUMPSIT

Assumpsit means simply "s/he promised."[12] In order to understand how the word is used in contract law it is first necessary to understand some legal history.

Very early in the history of English common law there were a small number of what were called "forms of action." If the circumstances of the plaintiff's complaint did not conform to the strictures of one of these "forms of action," the court would not grant the plaintiff redress. This system made matters rather tidy for the courts but left a lot of plaintiffs in unfortunate circumstances. The only forms of action available in contract cases were where the contract was under seal (covenant) or situations in which a person had promised to pay a sum certain in return for specific goods or services (debt). However, if, for example, Tim the shoemaker agreed to make a pair of shoes for Jack the farmer, unless Jack promised to pay Tim a specific amount of money, once Tim had made the shoes and Jack had walked off in them, Tim was out of luck because Jack had not expressly promised to pay a sum certain. Eventually, the common law courts began recognizing a form of action which they called *assumpsit*.[13] Originally, the courts only recognized *assumpsit* where the plaintiff alleged that the defendant had promised twice: once when making the initial contract and again upon acknowledging to the plaintiff that s/he did, indeed, owe him/her (the plaintiff) money. The word *assumpsit*, in this case, was deemed by the court to refer to the second, new, or acknowledging promise, not to the original contractual promise. The major breakthrough for plaintiffs suing on a theory of *assumpsit* came in *Slade's Case*.[14] In *Slade's Case*, the court decided that the promise signified by the word *assumpsit* was the promise in the original bargain. Thereafter, a defendant was unable to successfully defend his/her case by showing that s/he had not made a new promise. Courts soon began to expand the scope of *assumpsit*. Consequently, as Professor Allan Farnsworth has observed, "Over the course of the fifteenth and sixteenth centuries, the common law courts had thus succeeded in developing the action of *assumpsit* into a general basis for enforcing promises, including purely executory exchanges of promises."[15]

BONA FIDES

The phrase *bona fides* means "good faith."[16]

The UCC § 1-201(19) defines "good faith" as "honesty in fact in the conduct or transaction concerned." Section 2-103(1)(b) imposes a stricter standard of "good faith" for someone who is a "merchant."[17] This section further provides that, "good faith" in the case of a merchant means honesty in fact and the observance of reasonable commercial standards of fair dealing in the trade."

Thus, if I sell you my used golf clubs at a tag-sale in my front yard, I am not held to the same standard of good faith as the saleswoman at a golf discount warehouse when she sells a new set of clubs. She, unlike me, is charged with observing reasonable commercial standards of fair dealing in the trade. I, on the other hand, could tell you all sorts of stupid things about my clubs and still be acting in good faith so long as I was really being honest about it. The saleswoman, however, probably cannot get away with being stupid about golf clubs without being unreasonable with respect to commercial standards.

The UCC § 1-203, captioned "Obligation of Good Faith," provides that "Every contract or duty within this Act [i.e., the UCC] imposes an obligation of good faith in its performance or enforcement." Similarly, the Restatement (Second) of Contracts § 205 states that "[e]very contract imposes upon each party a duty of good faith and fair dealing in its performance and its enforcement."

CAVEAT EMPTOR

Caveat emptor is translated "let the buyer be on his/her guard" or, as it is commonly translated, "let the buyer beware."[18]

Before modern times and the vast amount of legislation which has been passed in order to protect consumers, the rule of *caveat emptor* reigned. A buyer, in order to protect him/herself, had to carefully inspect goods or carefully investigate the references of someone whom s/he wished to hire to perform services. Before today's consumer protection laws and unfair trade practices acts, a buyer was at great risk in the marketplace. Of course, when s/he has the time, energy, and inclination, it is still prudent for a buyer to carefully inspect goods and inquire about the quality of services before contracting to buy. Nevertheless, the consumer protection laws of today impose a host of implied warranties on a seller (especially a merchant). Furthermore, modern notions of strict liability and products liability impose other obligations and liabilities on manufacturers and sellers as well.

Modern legislation which regulates the sales of securities was designed to abolish the burden of *caveat emptor* on consumers of securities.[19] In *S.E.C. v. Capital Gains Bureau*,[20] Justice Goldberg commented that "a fundamental purpose" of our securities statutes "was to substitute a philosophy of full disclosure for the philosophy of *caveat emptor* and thus to achieve a high standard of business ethics in the securities industry."[21]

NUDUM PACTUM

The phrase *nudum pactum* means "a naked agreement."[22] In the language of the law, a *pactum* is considered *nudum* when the agreement lacks consideration.

In order for a contract to be valid, there must be consideration. The parties must exchange one thing for another in order for consideration to be present.[23] The "bargain theory" of consideration holds that, so long as each party actually intends to exchange the thing which s/he has for the thing which the other party has, that, in and of itself, is sufficient to constitute consideration.[24] An exchange of one party's promise for the other party's promise is almost always sufficient for consideration.

Therefore, in cases where the court determines that there was, in fact, no consideration, whatever agreement was made was not a contract but instead merely a *nudum pactum* (i.e., an agreement unsupported by consideration). Some cases are readily identifiable as lacking consideration. For example, if Farmer A and Farmer B agree that Farmer A will give Farmer B any surplus milk at the end of every business day and that Farmer B need not do anything in return, it is clear that such an agreement is merely a *nudum pactum*, for want of consideration.

There are, however, far more subtle ways in which an agreement might become a *nudum pactum*. One way involves what has come to be known as the "pre-existing duty" rule. For example, Restatement (Second) of Contracts § 73 illustration no. 4 states:

> A, an architect, agrees with B to superintend a construction project for a fixed fee. During the course of the project, without excuse, A takes away his plans and refuses to continue, and B promises him an extra fee if A will resume work. A's resumption of work is not consideration for B's promise of an extra fee.

Thus, the second agreement between A and B was a *nudum pactum*. Under their original agreement, B was already obligated to superintend the project (i.e., he had a pre-existing duty to superintend the project).[25]

"Past" consideration is another common way that an agreement can become a *nudum pactum* instead of a contract supported by consideration. One of the most famous "past" consideration cases is *Mills v. Wyman*.[26] Mills paid the expenses of and took care of the sick Wyman for a little over two weeks. Shortly thereafter, Wyman's father wrote Mills thanking him and promising to pay him for his expenses. The court held that Wyman's promise to pay expenses was a *nudum pactum* because Mills had performed his services and incurred his expenses before Wyman promised to pay.[27] There could be no consideration because the parties had not exchanged one promise for another.

Cases such as these can be disconcerting. Often the parties think that they are making a valid contract and intend to be bound by their agreement. However, there are instances in which a *nudum pactum* can be enforced. Sections 82 through 89 of the Restatement (Second) of Contracts enumerate several types of *nuda pacta* which can, under certain circumstances, be enforceable.[28]

QUANTUM MERUIT

After *Slade's Case*,[29] *assumpsit* became an important action in the common law courts. There were three "common counts" of *assumpsit*: debt, *quantum meruit*, and *quantum valebat*. Debt arose from lending money. *Quantum meruit* arose from performance of services. *Quantum valebat* arose from a sale of goods.

The phrase *quantum meruit* means "How much did s/he/it deserve?"[30] This term is the cornerstone of the law of restitution. In contracts class in law school, students usually study a variety of cases in which there was, in fact, no contract formed.[31] In those situations, the plaintiff usually seeks restitution. The law of restitution is principally interested in preventing one party from being unjustly enriched at the expense of another. If, for example, a doctor happened upon the scene of an auto accident and came to the aid of an unconscious victim; although there was no contract involved (since the victim was unconscious it is clear that there was no offer and acceptance), the victim would still be liable for the reasonable value of the physician's services. If the victim were not legally bound to pay for the reasonable value of the doctor's services, s/he (the victim) would be unjustly enriched by the doctor's work. Therefore, the doctor could sue the victim (or, and we hope that this is not the case, the victim's estate) on a theory of *quantum meruit*. S/he conferred a benefit on the victim, and is entitled to restitution in the amount that s/he deserved[32]

Restitution, in the form of *quantum meruit*, is also recoverable by a plaintiff for breach of contract.[33] If one party to a contract commits a material breach while the other party is still in the process of performing his/her duties pursuant to the contract, the non-breaching party may rescind the contract and ask for damages based on a theory of *quantum meruit*—the amount which the non-breaching party had spent in materials and labor prior to the breach by the other party.

QUASI EX CONTRACTU

In Latin this phrase simply means "as if out of contract." As was discussed above, lawyers tend to lump together with contract cases those cases in which, for one reason or another, no valid contract exists.[34] In many of those cases, especially where one party has conferred a benefit on the other (i.e., one party has been unjustly enriched at the other's expense), the law allows recovery based on rights under a theory of *quasi ex contractu*, or, more simply, quasi-contract.

There are two basic types of situations which give rise to suits in quasi-contract. One type is the type described above in which the doctor provided medical services for an injured accident victim.[35] Although no contract exists between the doctor and the victim, the doctor is still able to recover (in quasi-contract) the reasonable value of his/her services (*quantum meruit*). The classic example of this type of case is *Cotnam v. Wisdom*.[36] In *Cotnam v. Wisdom* the accident victim actually died and, thus, there was a question as to whether the victim had received any benefit. The court held that the victim's death was irrelevant to the physician's ability to prevail on the issue of damages.[37] The doctor was entitled to the "reasonable and customary price" for services rendered.[38] Secondly, in many cases where the contract is unenforceable or void *ab initio*,[39] an aggrieved party may seek recovery based upon a theory of quasi-contract.

There is no rule which limits the amount which a plaintiff may recover, in a suit based on quasi-contract, to restitution. Nevertheless, it is unusual for courts to award damages which exceed *quantum meruit* in quasi-contract suits. Restitution is the rule in quasi-contract; expectation damages or reliance damages, the exception.

QUID PRO QUO

In Latin, *quid pro quo* literally means "what for what?" It is also often translated "something for something." The phrase *quid pro quo* is a shorthand way of expressing the concept of consideration.[40] In Anglo-American law, valid contracts must have consideration. A gratuitous promise is not considered a valid contract because the party who is to receive the benefit of the gratuitous promise gives nothing for what the promising party offers. Similarly, there can be a failure of consideration because of the pre-existing duty rule or the rule regarding "past" consideration.[41]

In an elementary sense, consideration is the existence of a mutual exchange between the parties. In most contracts, parties exchange promises. Each promise is premised upon the contingency of the other's promise.[42]

Although the Restatement (Second) of Contracts § 90 renders lack of consideration a less potent defense against a plaintiff than it would be otherwise, the absence of a *quid pro quo* generally can still help a defendant limit damages to restitution (*quantum meruit*) as opposed to expectation. Hence, the presence or absence of a *quid pro quo* (i.e., the presence or absence of consideration) is still an important issue in real-life contracts cases and in law school examination questions.

■ ENDNOTES

1. *Ab* is a preposition meaning "from" and *initio* is the ablative singular of *initium* ("the beginning").

2. Generally one of the parties has not kept his/her promise (i.e., has breached the contract) and the non-breaching party, as plaintiff, sues the defendant, breaching party.

3. This is specific performance—a relatively unusual remedy except in cases involving something unique, like the sale of land.

4. Expectation damages. *See* Restatement (Second) of Contracts § 347 (1981). *Also see Hadley v. Baxendale,* 9 Ex. 341, 156 Eng. Rep. 145 (1859).

5. I say "generally" because the Restatement (Second) of Contracts § 90 allows a court to award expectation damages even where a contract is otherwise void or unenforceable in cases where the plaintiff has reasonably relied on the defendant's promise to his/her (the plaintiff's) detriment.

6. *See quid pro quo, infra.*

7. In early Roman law duress of this nature did not bother the Romans. Not because they did not have revolvers (substitute a dagger held to the throat if anachronism bothers you) but because of the principle "*Coactus voluit, tamen voluit*," meaning "Although he was coerced when he agreed, nevertheless, he agreed." Later in the Empire, they softened this hard-line position, recognizing duress as a defense.

8. *See* M. Walzer, Spheres of Justice 100-103 (1983).

9. It is virtually impossible for a high school Latin student to escape two years of studying the language without hearing the famous phrase, "*Iacta alea est*," which is universally translated "the die is cast." According to Suetonius, Julius Caesar spoke those words upon crossing the Rubicon with his army in January of 49 B.C. The Rubicon was the southernmost boundary between Cisalpine Gaul (where Caesar had been governor since 58 B.C.) and Italy. For a Roman governor to enter Italy with armed troops was not only bad manners but illegal as well. By entering Italy in this fashion, Caesar plunged Rome into a bloody civil war. War in many respects is the ultimate game of chance. Caesar's statement, "*Iacta alea est*," suggests that he was

aware of the significance of his actions. Like dice, Caesar had tossed his future and the fate of Rome to chance.

10. However, even when performance is dependent upon a fortuitous event, if the performance of both parties is dependent upon the same event, that agreement is not considered an aleatory contract. For example, if I say to you, "I'll mow your lawn for $10 on Saturday if it doesn't rain" and you answer "OK, I'll pay you $10 to mow my lawn on Saturday," it is clear that both my performance (mowing) and yours (paying me $10) are contingent upon the same fortuitous event (i.e., that it not rain on Saturday). An absence of rain on Saturday is a condition precedent to performance but it does not make our contract an aleatory one simply because it is dependent upon chance.

11. A material breach by one party ordinarily constitutes sufficient grounds for the other party to consider his/her duties under the contract as discharged. Illustration 1 to § 379 of the Restatement (Second) of Contracts illustrates the point well:

> A, an insurance company, issues to B a policy of fire insurance on B's house for a year in the amount of $100.00. In consideration, B gives A his promissory note for the premium, payable in three months. B fails to pay the note at maturity. Four months later, before A has given notice of cancellation, B's house burns. A cannot treat B's failure to pay as discharging it from its duty to pay for the loss under the policy. A is liable for the loss less the amount of the note.

12. One of the most famous cases in contract law is *Hawkins v. McGee*, 84 N.H. 114, 146 A.641 (1929), which involves a doctor, McGee, who guaranteed that he could surgically repair George Hawkins's hand (George had burned his hand on an electric wire when he was eleven) and thus make it "a hundred percent good hand." Unfortunately the good Dr. McGee grafted skin from George's chest onto his hand resulting in a hand which was not only burned and scarred but hairy as well. *Hawkins v. McGee* was the very first contracts case which I read in law school. And the very first sentence of that case reads as follows: "Assumpsit against a surgeon for breach of an alleged warranty of the success of an operation." Thus, the very first word which I read in contracts class was *assumpsit*.

The Latin verb *assumere* means "to take up, receive, adopt, accept, take." In the sense in which it is used in the law, it means something a bit more like "to accept as one's burden" or "to take on one's own account." We probably should interpret it to mean "promise." The form *assumpsit* is the third-person singular perfect tense.

13. The plaintiff alleged that the defendant "promised" to pay—even if no specific amount had been decided upon.

14. 76 Eng. Rep. 1074 (1602).

15. E. A. Farnsworth, Contracts 19-20 (1982).

16. There are two Latin words spelled f-i-d-e-s. One type of *fides* is a string for a musical instrument; the other *fides* means "trust, confidence, reliance, credence, belief, faith." When you encounter the term *bona fides* in legal writing, the author will be using the latter of the two (i.e, "trust, confidence, etc."). The Latin adjective *bona* simply means "good." The case *Smith v. Zimbalist*, 2 Cal. App. 2d 324, 38 P.2d 170 (1934), involved a sale of two supposedly rare (one Guarnerius and one Stradivarius) violins. *Smith v. Zimbalist* is often used to illustrate problems of mistake or warranty. This is the only case I know of in which the plaintiff complains that the defendant did not give him as *bona fides* (as good a gut string) as the plaintiff had hoped (using the first meaning of f-i-d-e-s).

17. The UCC § 2-104(1) defines "merchant" as follows:

> "Merchant" means a person who deals in goods of the kind or otherwise by his occupation holds himself out as having knowledge or skill peculiar to the practices or goods involved in the transaction or to whom such knowledge or skill may be attributed by his employment of an agent or broker or other intermediary who by his occupation holds himself out as having such knowledge or skill.

18. It is difficult to go through life, much less law school, without hearing the phrase *caveat emptor. Caveat* is the third-person singular present active subjunctive form of the Latin verb *cave cavēre* ("to be on one's guard, to guard against, to beware"), and as such means "let him/her be on his/her guard." *Cavēre* is also the verb found in the familiar phrase *cave canem* ("beware of the dog."). *Emptor* is the Latin noun meaning "a buyer, purchaser."

19. *See,* e.g., The Securities Exchange Act of 1934. 15 U.S.C. § 78 (a) (1988) *et seq.*

20. 376 U.S. 180 (1963).

21. *Id.* at 186.

22. The Latin noun *pactum* comes directly from the verb *paciscor* which means "to make a bargain" or "to make an agreement." Hence, the noun *pactum* means "an agreement, covenant, treaty, pact." The adjective *nudum* simply means "naked, unclothed, bare."

23. *See* the discussion in *Ab Initio, supra,* and in *Quid Pro Quo, infra.*

24. *See generally* E. A. Farnsworth, *supra, note* 15 at 41-82 (1982).

25. In the actual case upon which the Restatement illustration is based, *Lingenfelder v. Wainwright Brewing Co.*, 103 Mo. 578, 15 S.W. 844 (1891), the court stated,

> What we hold is that, when a party merely does what he has already obligated himself to do, he cannot demand an additional compensation therefor, and although by taking advantage of the

necessities of his adversary [i.e., the other party to the contract], he obtains a promise for more, the law will regard it as *nudum pactum*, and will not lend its process to aid in the wrong.

15 S.W. 844, 848.

26. 3 Pick. (20 Mass.) 207 (1825).

27. *Id.* at 211.

28. For example, § 82 provides that, if a person promises to pay a debt which would be enforceable if it were not for the statute of limitations having run, such a promise is binding. And of course, § 90 (discussed briefly *supra* in *Ab Initio*) also makes it possible for a court to enforce a *nudum pactum* in cases involving detrimental reliance, which is reasonable.

29. *See Assumpsit, supra.*

30. The Latin word *quantum* is a substantive form of the interrogative adjective *quantus*. As such, *quantum* means "how much?" *Meruit* is the third-person singular perfect active tense of the Latin verb *merere* ("to deserve," "to earn") and, thus, means "s/he/it deserved."

31. Generally called "quasi-contract"; *see Quasi Ex Contractu, infra.*

32. That is, the reasonable value of his/her services to the victim; generally an amount equal to that which the defendant would have to pay to acquire the plaintiff's performance. *See* Restatement (Second) of Contracts § 371(a) (1981).

33. That is, Restitution is not *only* available to a plaintiff in quasi-contract.

34. *See Quantum Meruit, supra.*

35. *Id.*

36. 83 Ark. 601, 104 S.W. 164 (1907).

37. *Id.* at 605, 104 S.W. at 166. One could say that merely because the victim didn't recover did not bar the doctor from recovering.

38. *Id.*

39. *See generally Ab Initio, supra.*

40. *See* discussion of "consideration" at *Ab Initio, supra* and *Nudum Pactum, supra.*

41. *See* discussion in *Nudum Pactum, supra.*

42. In his dissent in *Kaiser Steel Corp. v. Mullins*, 455 U.S. 72 (1982), Justice Brennan explained why the contract at issue was supported by consideration as follows:

Kaiser Steel Corporation and The United Mine Workers (UMW) entered into a collective bargaining agreement in 1974. As part of that agreement, Kaiser promised to make contributions to certain UMW-designated employee health and retirement plan funds, based in part upon the amount of coal purchased by Kaiser from non-UMW mines. This purchased-coal clause obviously had value to Kaiser's UMW employees, because the agreement provided that if the clause were adjudged illegal, then the union could demand renegotiation of the contract in order to secure a *quid pro quo* for the invalidated clause.

Id. at 89-90.

CHAPTER FOUR

CORPORATIONS AND TAX

■ THE ROMAN BACKGROUND

Ancient Roman law recognized several different types of entities which are somewhat analogous to our modern business organizations. The most well known among Roman juristic persons was the "state" itself, the Populus Romanus. In addition, certain subdivisions of the state such as *municipia* and *civitates* (i.e., municipalities) also took on corporate form. Furthermore, there were a number of private business organizations that operated in ancient Rome. Scholars debate whether all of these associations had corporate capacity (i.e., status as a legal entity). Nevertheless, it appears as though the Romans did recognize the fundamental concept of a corporate juristic person that was, in many respects, distinct from the individuals who comprised it. *Sodalitates* were associations that primarily conducted ancient and state-sponsored cults. The most common private business organizations were the *collegia*, many of which functioned like trade guilds. Apparently, the *collegia* did not acquire corporate entity status until the time of Marcus Aurelius (c. 180 A.D.). Under Roman law, corporations generally had to be authorized by the state (a requirement adopted by modern corporate law as well) and had broad powers to govern themselves. The Romans did not, however, view these corporations as entirely divorced from their members. For example, although a corporation could sue and be sued in Roman courts and could own property, if all of its current members died, the corporation, too, ceased to exist. The Romans also had certain charitable organizations called *piae causae* that had many of the characteristics of modern non-profit organizations.

In addition to the business organizations that possessed varying degrees of corporate personality, the ancient Romans utilized partnerships as well. A Roman partnership, or *societas,* was composed of at least two individuals who combined their resources in an effort to achieve a common goal. A contract was all that was necessary to form a *societas* and, unlike the *collegia,* a *societas* did not have to obtain state approval.

Romans had a number of taxes throughout antiquity. Roman citizens paid two types of taxes that were vital to the well-being of the state: a direct property tax (*tributum soli*) and a poll tax (*tributum capitis*). The *tributum soli* was a tax assessed mostly to generate revenue in times of emergency, such as the Second Punic War in the late third century B.C. Romans also paid a relatively minor customs duty.

American corporations and tax laws today are voluminous and incredibly complex. All states have enacted statutes that govern the formation and operation of corporations, partnerships, and limited partnerships. These statutes typically establish filing and reporting procedures and provide mechanisms by which businesses may function. Federal laws such as the Securities Act of 1933 and the Williams Act govern the sale of corporate securities. A host of other state and federal laws affect business operations either directly or indirectly. The Internal Revenue Code and its attendant regulations are among the most intricate statutes ever devised. In addition to income taxes, we also pay sales and use taxes, property taxes, gift taxes, inheritance taxes, and others. Our tax structure is essentially progressive in nature.

AD VALOREM

This phrase simply means "in accordance with value."[1] An *ad valorem* tax is levied on the value or worth of the specific real or personal property subject to taxation.[2] The most common method of assessing property taxes is *ad valorem.* Property owners typically pay a tax on their houses, automobiles, and personal property to their town or municipality based upon the appraised value of those items. Town tax assessors inspect homes in order to determine an assessment or valuation of the property. Automobiles are regularly given a standard value based upon the brand and age of the car. The concept of an *ad valorem* tax is rather elementary. The fundamental precept is that individuals who own expensive property are better able to afford a higher tax than those who own less costly real estate or personalty. A person who owns a $200,000 house must pay a higher *ad valorem* property tax than someone who owns a $75,000 condominium.

In addition to property taxes, there are other types of taxes which are assessed on an *ad valorem* basis as well. For example, estate and gift taxes are based upon the value of the property given by a decedent. Inheritance taxes also are based upon the worth of property inherited.

ALTER EGO

Alter ego literally means "a second I" or more loosely "a second self."[3]

Legal writers use the term *alter ego* with respect to primarily two issues in a corporate law context: namely, certain actions of promoters and certain conduct undertaken by shareholders.

When individuals begin planning to establish a corporation, we call those persons "promoters."[4] Promoters typically conceive the idea for starting the business, study the problems associated with such an undertaking (e.g., financing, real estate, employment, suppliers, etc.), plan and coordinate the business's inception (often involving legal considerations), and then, more often than not, actually begin operating the new enterprise. When promoters engage in the myriad activities associated with launching a corporation, it is technically impossible for them to be acting on behalf of the corporation, since the corporation itself does not yet exist at that time. However, as a general rule of the law of corporations, the incipient corporation is deemed the *alter ego* of a promoter.[5] Therefore, when a promoter executes a contract with a third party (for example, a promoter could sign a lease for office space, furniture, computer equipment, etc.), if the corporate entity does, in fact, come into existence by virtue of signing and filing the appropriate certificate of incorporation and paying the required fees, then the executed contract may become the obligation of the corporation, not the individual promoter. The corporation, however, must indicate (either expressly or implicitly) that it wishes to be bound by the promoter's agreement. One legal theory that allows a corporation to automatically step into the promoter's contractual shoes is that the corporation is merely the *alter ego*, or "second self," of the promoter.[6]

Perhaps the most well-known circumstance in which courts invoke the *alter ego* principle in a corporate context is when a party seeks to "pierce the corporate veil." One of the fundamental tenets of corporations law is the notion of limited liability for shareholders.[7] Corporate shareholders, as investors, are only liable to creditors of the corporation up to the amount of their investment (i.e., the subscription price of the shares they have purchased).[8] Clearly, the doctrine of limited liability is partially responsible for so many people choosing the corporate form when beginning a business.[9] Courts have, however, refused to permit the mere existence of a corporate facade to shield fraud or other culpable activity when the corporation is the *alter ego* of one or a few shareholders responsible for wrongful conduct.[10] Generally courts apply the *alter ego* doctrine and allow piercing the corporate veil when a corporation with few shareholders commits some type of fraud, fails to pay dividends, fails to observe corporate formalities (e.g., holding annual meetings, keeping proper records), or begins business while grossly undercapitalized.[11]

In such circumstances, courts say that the corporation is the *alter ego* or "instrumentality" of the shareholder(s) and, thus, hold the shareholder(s) liable for the injuries they have caused by their misconduct. However, Professor Clark emphasizes that the tyrannical or oligarchical control by one or a small number of shareholders renders those stockholders liable for the corporation's debts under the *alter ego* doctrine only "when they have caused it [the corporation] to commit a 'fraud or wrong.' "[12] Thus, a corporation does not ordinarily become equated with its stockholders. The *alter ego* doctrine is, therefore, an exception to the general rule of limited liability for corporate shareholders.[13]

PAR

Par is the Latin adjective that means "equal, matching in magnitude or intensity."

Corporate lawyers use the word *par* when referring to a special kind of stock, namely *par* value stock. Although many states still allow corporations to issue shares with *par* value, the trend in modern business practice is moving away from shares with *par* value. In fact, in 1979 the American Bar Association–American Law Institute excised the sections of the Model Business Corporation Act that had dealt with *par* value.[14] Nevertheless, since untold numbers of corporations still function with *par* value stock, it is important for attorneys who deal with corporations to be familiar with the concept of "equal value stock."

To begin with, a company arbitrarily establishes what the *par* value of its stock will be in its articles of incorporation. It is not uncommon for companies to set *par* value at one dollar, one cent, or even a fraction of a cent. Companies have traditionally set *par* value very low both for tax reasons and so that on the market the stock will ordinarily sell well above *par*.[15]

The basic premise of *par* value is this: when a corporation is just beginning to issue shares, it will sell them all at the same (*par* value) price. Theoretically, when a corporation sells shares at *par* value, each new stockholder can rest assured that s/he will not be buying shares at a price higher than other investors. Historically, the practice of selling stock at *par* value, then, insured equal standing and treatment for all initial shareholders in a company. By the same token, the existence of an established *par* value should allow the company's creditors, at least in theory, to know more precisely the value of the company's assets.[16]

Human ingenuity, however, has functionally dismantled these traditional functions of *par* value stock. For example, since it is permissible in some states to buy stock with non-cash property, promissory notes, or even a promise of future services,[17] it is not necessarily possible for a shareholder to be certain that s/he is paying a price equal to that which other shareholders are paying for *par* value stock. The practice of issuing shares for no consideration, so-called "bonus" shares, has also contributed to the demise of *par* value stock. Similarly, corporations have been known to sell *par* value shares for less than *par* value and characterize them as "discount" shares. In addition, when companies issue stock for services, where the objective value of those services rendered is actually below *par* value, such sales of what has come to be known as "watered" stock defeat the original intent of establishing a *par* value.[18] When companies issue bonus, discount, or watered shares, *par* value becomes virtually meaningless in terms of guaranteeing equality among shareholders or guaranteeing the asset value of a corporation for creditors.

Modern corporation statutes have adapted (at least for the time being) to the realities of dealing with the troublesome aspects of *par*, no-*par*, bonus, discount, and watered stocks.[19] No doubt, creative promoters will devise new and imaginative schemes for issuing stocks that will soon send the courts and legislators back to the drawing board in order to maintain equities among shareholders and protect the legitimate interests of the public.

PRO RATA

The term *pro rata*, meaning "in relation to fixed proportions," occurs frequently both in corporate as well as tax law.[20] One of the most attractive features of corporations for investors is that for-profit corporations routinely pay dividends to their shareholders.[21] Whether the company pays dividends in cash, property, or additional stock, those dividends are customarily paid on a *pro rata* basis. In other words, the dividend amount distributed to each shareholder is dependent upon the number of shares that the shareholder owns. For example, if a company pays a cash dividend and determines that the dividend shall be $2 per share, a person who owns 100 shares would receive $200. The dividends are, therefore, in relation to the number of shares owned by the individual.

One aspect of receiving dividends that most shareholders find distasteful is the income tax consequence. When shareholders get dividends, the IRS treats those dividends as ordinary income for tax purposes. However, through repurchases and redemptions of stock, corporations are able to provide shareholders with payments for stock that the IRS will treat as capital gains (and therefore the shareholder pays a lower tax than s/he would if the IRS were to treat the transaction as creating ordinary income instead of capital gains). Both redemptions and repurchases involve a corporation buying stock back from shareholders.[22]

Of course, when a shareholder sells stock, the IRS treats whatever profit (if any) the shareholder makes on such a sale of a security as a capital gain. And, as a capital gain, the amount that the seller realizes from the sale is taxed at a lower rate than if that profit were characterized as ordinary income. It is mechanically possible for a company to buy stock back from its shareholders (either through redemptions or repurchases) on a *pro rata* basis. However, when a corporation redeems or repurchases stock from its shareholders in proportion to the number of shares owned (i.e., on a *pro rata* basis), the IRS, smelling a rat, ignores the ostensible repurchase or redemption facade and taxes the individual shareholders as if they had received dividends (i.e., as if the sale of stock had created ordinary income).[23]

QUORUM

Quorum, strictly speaking, means "whose" or "of whom."[24] The English language now employs the word *quorum* to refer to the minimum number of group members necessary for that group to make valid and binding decisions. Organizations being what they are, it is nearly impossible to assemble 100% of the members of any group for purposes of making decisions. Consequently, many organizations provide that, if a certain fixed number of members (i.e., a *quorum*) is present and capable of participating in the decision-making process, then those decisions made by that (less than 100%) body will be valid and binding on the entire group. The organization members, in essence, agree that decisions made by the group, at least a minimum number "of whom" are present for the vote, will be valid.

Normally, a number of group structures exist within any corporation: the board of directors; the corporate officers; and, the shareholders being the most obvious discernible groups. To be sure, the directors, corporate officers, and shareholders typically are the groups who make business decisions on behalf of the corporation. The articles of incorporation and bylaws ordinarily establish which groups within a corporation will make certain types of decisions.

In order for decisions made by shareholders at shareholders' meetings to be valid, a *quorum* must be present at the meeting. Similarly, in order for decisions made by directors at board meetings to be valid, a *quorum* of directors is required. A *quorum* rule is necessary to prevent a forceful minority from seizing control.

The bylaws of a corporation typically establish what the *quorum* will be for a meeting of shareholders. Statutes, however, may dictate certain limits. For example, the Model Business Corporation Act (MBCA) provides that a corporation may not set its *quorum* for meetings of shareholders at less than one-third of shares entitled to vote.[25] A statute may also fill the gap in the event that neither the articles of incorporation nor the bylaws of a corporation set the *quorum* number. The MBCA uses a majority of shares entitled to vote as a *quorum*.[26] As a general rule, a simple majority vote is effective when a *quorum* is present.[27]

Quorum requirements also apply to meetings of the board of directors of a corporation. A corporation's bylaws usually define what constitutes a *quorum* of the board of directors. In the absence of such a provision, statutes generally provide that a majority of directors constitutes a *quorum*.[28] Many states prohibit a corporation from defining the *quorum* of its board as less than one-third of the board's members.[29] As is the case with meetings of shareholders, if a *quorum* is present at a board meeting, a majority vote of those present is valid and binding with the same practical effect as if the entire board had voted unanimously.[30]

The *quorum* principle, as it relates to shareholders' meetings and meetings of a board of directors, is designed to promote fairness. When groups which comprise various component parts of a business make decisions, *quorum* requirements ensure that a significant number of the relevant groups are the ones who make those decisions.

ULTRA VIRES

Ultra vires means "beyond the powers."[31] In *McDermott v. Bear Film Co.*, the court explained the doctrine of *ultra vires* as follows: "In its true sense the phrase *ultra vires* describes action which is beyond the purpose or power of the corporation. . . . Some courts have inflated the phrase to characterize acts which are within corporate purpose or power but performed in an unauthorized manner or without authority."[32]

Today modern corporations' statutes generally allow corporations to do just about everything that natural persons can do.[33] This was not always true. "Early corporate statutes expressly granted limited powers to corporations and allowed them to engage only in certain specified lines of business."[34] Consequently, when corporations performed acts which were outside of the scope of activity prescribed in the corporation's articles of incorporation or bylaws (e.g., executed contracts or committed torts or crimes), courts had to determine whether to hold corporations liable for conduct that was technically beyond the corporation's powers.

The paradigm case that illustrates the *ultra vires* doctrine is *Ashbury Railway Carriage & Iron Co. v. Riche*.[35] The company's charter stated that its purpose was to "sell or lend all kinds of railway plant, to carry on the business of mechanical engineers and general contractors, & c." Ashbury Railway, however, contracted with Riche to build and operate a Belgian railroad. When Ashbury repudiated the contract after initially undertaking performance, Riche sued. The House of Lords held that Riche could not recover from the corporation because the company's charter did not permit it to construct and run a railroad in Belgium. Lord Chancellor Cairns stated, "this contract was . . . entirely beyond the objects of the memorandum of association." He therefore reasoned that Ashbury's contract with Riche was "void at its beginning . . . because the company could not make the contract."

As was noted above, the modern view is that corporations have extremely broad powers. In fact, when drafting articles of incorporation for corporations today, although they may actually state the particular purpose of the corporation (e.g., to manufacture and sell plush toys), most attorneys include a catch-all clause stating, for example, "or to perform such other lawful acts as its members or board of directors may from time to time deem useful or appropriate." Today's Model Business Corporation Act specifically provides that the *ultra vires* doctrine may be invoked to challenge the validity of a corporate action in three narrow circumstances: (1) when a shareholder sues the corporation seeking an injunction; (2) "in a proceeding by the corporation, directly, derivatively, or through a receiver, trustee, or other legal representative, against an incumbent or former director, officer, employee, or agent of the corporation"; or (3) when the attorney general brings a suit against the corporation pursuant to a specific section of the Model Business Corporation Act.[36] Thus, as regards the powers of a corporation, because of the limited applications of the doctrine, *ultra vires* is not as important as it once was.

The doctrine of *ultra vires* is relevant, however, in terms of conduct that is and is not authorized for directors and officers of a corporation. For example, the articles of incorporation or bylaws may specify the powers of the corporate secretary. If a secretary were to perform a duty that the bylaws had delegated only to the president, such conduct could be characterized as *ultra vires* (i.e., beyond the powers of his/her particular office). In such circumstances, the officer who acted *ultra vires* would be personally liable for whatever damage or injury s/he caused by acting outside of the scope of his/her duties.[37]

■ ENDNOTES

1. *Ad* is a preposition meaning, here, "in accordance with" or "in proportion to." *Valorem* is the accusative singular noun formed from the verb "valere" ("to be equivalent in value to" or "to be worth"), and thus is the object of the preposition *ad* and means "value" or "worth."

2. *See* 84 C.J.S. *Taxation* § 3 n.50 (1954).

3. *Alter* is an adjective meaning "a second, further, another." *Ego* is the first-person singular pronoun in the nominative case meaning "I." Sigmund Freud identified the *ego* as one of the three dimensions of human personality (the other two being the *id* and the *superego*). In doing so, Freud referred to the *ego* as the "self" and consequently put a minor twist into our popular, modern definition of this Latin pronoun.

4. *See generally* H. Henn and J. Alexander, Laws of Corporations 236 *et seq.* (1983).

5. *Id.* at 257.

6. Other theories are also applicable (e.g., ratification, assignment, third-party beneficiary, etc.). *See id.* at 252-257.

7. *See generally* R. Clark, Corporate Law 7 (1986).

8. *Id.*

9. *Id.* at 27.

10. *See generally* 18 Am. Jur. 2d *Corporations* §45 (1985).

11. *DeWitt Truck Brokers v. W. Ray Flemming Fruit Co.*, 540 F. 2d 681, 686-87 (4th Cir. 1976). In *Minton v. Cavaney*, 364 P.2d 473, 475 (1961), Justice Traynor commented on the *alter ego* doctrine as follows:

> The figurative terminology "alter ego" and "disregard of the corporate entity" is generally used to refer to the various situations that are an abuse of corporate privilege. The equitable owners of a corporation, for example, are personally liable when they treat the assets of the corporation as their own and add or withdraw capital from the corporation at will; when they hold themselves out as being personally liable for the debts of the corporation; or when they provide inadequate capitalization and

actively participate in the conduct of corporate affairs. (Citations omitted).

12. R. Clark, *supra* note 7 at 37.

13. *See also* Barber, *Piercing the Corporate Veil,* 17 Willamette L. Rev. 371 (1981); Note, *Piercing the Corporate Veil: The Alter Ego Doctrine Under Federal Common Law,* 95 Harv. L. Rev. 853 (1982).

14. *See* H. Henn and J. Alexander, *supra,* note 4 at 283 n.2 (1983). All states allow corporations to issue no-*par* shares.

15. *H. Henn* and *J. Alexander, supra* note 4, at 283 n. 2.

16. In his popular casebook, Professor Hamilton remarks, "In effect, par value originally ensured proportionality of treatment of widely dispersed shareholders, increased confidence in the resale market that the shares being resold had real value (and were not 'mere pieces of paper'), and assured the population in general that corporations had been in fact capitalized as advertised by the par values of the shares they issued." R. Hamilton, Corporations 240 (1981).

17. *See* Model Business Corp. Act § 6.21(b) (1988). But note that a number of states (e.g. New York) prohibit the sale of stock using either a promissory note or an agreement to perform services in the future as consideration.

18. Courts, however, using various theories of trust, have imposed additional liabilities on holders of watered, bonus, and discount stock. *See e.g., Sawyer v. Hoag,* 84 U.S. 610 (1873); *Hospes v. Northwestern Mfg. & Car Co.,* 48 Minn. 174, 50 N.W. 1117 (1895); *Bing Crosby Minute Maid Corp. v. Eaton,* 297 P.2d 5 (1956); *DuPont v. Ball,* 106 A. 39 (Del. 1918). The Model Bus. Corp. Act, on the other hand, currently extends protection for owners of watered shares. *See* Model Business Corp. Act § 6.22(a).

19. *See* R. Clark, *supra* note 7, at 713 and R. Hamilton, *supra* note 16, at 245–48.

20. *Pro* is a preposition that has a number of meanings depending on context. Its most common meaning is probably "in front of" or "on behalf of." In this phrase, however, *pro* means "in relation to" or "in proportion to." *Rata* is the accusative neuter plural form of the adjective, *ratus, -a, -um* ("determined, fixed, certain, proportion"). Thus, *rata* literally means "things with a fixed proportion," or simply "fixed proportions."

21. Companies usually pay dividends from corporate earnings on a regular basis (e.g., quarterly). The board of directors makes the decision whether to pay dividends and the per share amount the company will pay.

22. Technically, a redemption involves a buy back of stock pursuant to a prearranged agreement (e.g. agreements in the articles of incorporation) while a repurchase typically occurs when a company simply buys back its own stock on the market. *See generally* R. Clark, *supra* note 7, at 625.

23. I.R.C. §§ 302(a), 302(b)(1), 301(a), 391(c) (1989).

24. *Quorum,* is the genitive plural (either masculine or feminine) of the relative pronoun *qui, quae, quod,* meaning "who" or "which." The genitive ordinarily denotes possession. In the instance of the relative pronoun, the genitive plural translates "whose" or "of whom."

In his *Commentaries,* Blackstone explained the word '*quorum*' as follows:

> The term *quorum* (literally, *of whom*) is one of the words used in England in the Latin form of the commission to justices of the peace. The part of the document wherein the word occurs reads thus: "We have assigned you, and every two or more of you, quorum aliquem vestrum, A, B, C, D, etc. *unum esse volumus,*—i.e., *of whom* we will that any one of you, A, B, or C, etc., shall be one." This made it necessary that certain individuals, who, in the language of the commission were said to be the *quorum,* should be present during the transaction of business.

Blackstone's Commentaries, I., 352.

25. Model Business Corp. Act § 32. (1988).

26. *Id.*

27. *Id.* Of course a corporation's articles of incorporation or bylaws may provide otherwise (e.g. with so-called "supermajority provisions").

28. *See e.g.,* Model Business Corp. Act § 8.24(a) (1988).

29. *See e.g.,* Del. Gen. Corp. Law § 141(b), McKinney's N.Y. Bus. Corp. Law § 707.

30. H. Henn and J. Alexander, *supra* note 4, at 569.

31. *Ultra* is an adjective meaning "beyond." *Vires* is the accusative plural (the object of the preposition *ultra*) form of the noun *vis, vis* (f.) meaning "physical strength" or "force." In the plural *vis* is normally translated as "physical powers" or simply "strength."

32. 219 Cal. App. 2d 607, 610, 33 Cal. Rptr. 486, 489 (1963).

33. Model Business Corp. Act §§ 3.01-3.02 (1988).

34. R. Clark, *supra* note 7, at 675.

35. 33 N.S. Law Times Rep. 450 (1875).

36. Model Business Corp. Act § 3.04 (1988).

37. H. Henn and J. Alexander, *supra* note 4, at 620.

CHAPTER FIVE

CRIMINAL LAW

■ THE ROMAN BACKGROUND

Criminal law in ancient Rome is a fascinating subject. A number of the best known Roman authors, such as Cicero, Tacitus, Pliny the Younger, and Suetonius, give us a vivid picture of some of the more juicy criminal trials.

Criminal law in the heyday of the Roman Republic (i.e., Cicero's day, roughly 140-40 B.C.) was strikingly different from the Criminal law of the bureaucratic empire which followed the Republic. By the late Republic, the Romans had established various permanent standing courts (*quaestiones perpetuae*) which handled certain specified criminal offenses. The juries were generally composed of people from the upper classes and the crimes with which the *quaestiones* were concerned were generally upper-class crimes. Each offense carried a standard, predetermined penalty. Thus, if the majority of the jury believed that the defendant was guilty, there was no need for a special hearing for sentencing; the jurors had no discretion regarding punishment. A special magistracy, the *tresviri capitales*, handled cases involving ordinary crime among the lower classes during the late Republic.

During the Roman Empire (particularly during the first and second centuries A.D.) the Romans dealt with criminal law quite differently. The senate took control of the most important upper class crimes (thus ousting some of the *quaestiones perpetuae*). Crimes no longer carried preordained punishments. Instead, the "juries" wielded great discretion in meting out punishment. And the punishments themselves tended to be more savage and brutal than the typical fines and banishment penalties imposed during the Republic.

Although criminal procedure changed significantly during the first and second centuries A.D., many of the crimes which had been subject to sanctions during the late Republic continued to be recognized as crimes in the early empire. The following list should provide a fair idea of the types of crimes recognized in ancient Roman criminal law.

Treason (*maiestas*) was one of the most important crimes often associated with the upper classes.

Extortion of money (*repetundae*) was a crime often perpetrated by Roman provincial governors.

Murder was a crime handled by a special murder court. That same court heard cases involving many other crimes including poisoning, arson, and castration.

The court for *vis publica* ("public power") handled crimes such as illegal possession of arms, false imprisonment, rape, prevention of burial, and court tampering.

Cases concerning illicit sexual activity, including adultery and incest, were administered by a special court called *de adulteriis*.

There were antitrust laws which prohibited fixing grain prices.

Ambitus, election bribery, was illegal. There were crimes similar to modern assault and battery. And, finally, there were a number of crimes involving tampering with documents and money (e.g., forgery, counterfeiting, etc.).

During the Empire, the emperors' bureaucracy created several new crimes such as blackmail (*concussio*), cattle-rustling (*abigeatus*), and burglary (*effractio*). And like all good authoritarian systems, the Empire created a crime called *stellionatus* (acting like a lizard). If the government wanted to charge you with a crime but couldn't find any better pretense, *stellionatus* would do just fine.

In the U.S. we have both state and federal criminal statutes which govern criminal conduct. Most federal crimes are predicated on the Commerce Clause of the Constitution. Federal law also affects state criminal laws by providing vital constitutional safeguards through the Bill of Rights. In law school, criminal law classes usually explore a variety of topics such as the purposes of criminal law, the nature of crime itself, and also specific types of crimes (e.g., murder, theft, robbery, conspiracy).

ACTUS REUS

In simple terms, *actus reus* means "an evil action."[1]

In order for the machinery of the criminal justice system to affect any specific problem, some person must cause harm in such a way that our society considers the harm which was caused to be of public importance. Society must prohibit the type of harm caused and the manner in which it was caused. Before the state imposes criminal sanctions on certain human conduct, we, as a society, must first determine that we wish to prohibit specific types of activity, and then identify those activities.

Although scholars have advanced numerous definitions for the phrase *actus reus*, J.W.C. Turner has posited a rather simple definition: "such result of human conduct as the law seeks to prevent."[2] Most criminal law scholars agree that crimes have both mental (i.e., subjective) elements and external (i.e., objective) elements.[3] In an elementary sense, the phrase *actus reus* refers to the external elements of a crime.

Therefore, the term *actus reus* refers to the deed or criminal conduct itself which society has chosen to prohibit. Whether the individual or individuals who perform a certain deed can be found guilty will also depend upon their mental state.[4]

Modern commentators have also observed that it is difficult to distinguish the criminal act itself from the circumstances surrounding the act: "*actus reus* includes circumstances and consequences, but that does not mean that an act must also be so inclusive. Even those who argue that acts are simply bodily movements would have to admit that acts are accompanied by circumstances and consequences."[5]

EX POST FACTO

The phrase *ex post facto* means "from after the deed" or "from after that which was done."[6]

For centuries Western Culture has advanced the principle that a person cannot be criminally liable for conduct which, at the time that s/he acted, was not illegal. The specific criminal law which the defendant is accused of having committed must have existed when the conduct in question occurred.

For example, suppose that on April 21, 1991, your state legislature passes a law changing the legal drinking age from 18 to 21 (making it illegal for anyone under the age of 21 to drink beer) and imposes a $500 fine on persons who violate the new law. Suppose that the legislature also declares that the new law shall be retroactive to April 1, 1991. In other words, the legislature intends the law to apply to persons under the age of 21 who drank beer at any time after April 1 (even though they did not pass the bill until the twenty-first). Such a criminal law would be *ex post facto* because it is intended to apply from after the time that persons have acted. For example, if you were 19 on April 7 and drank beer on that date, you would have been doing something which was entirely legal at that time. It runs counter to our sense of justice to allow a legislature to render that conduct criminal at a later date. People are expected to conform their actions to the criminal laws as they exist, not to the laws as they predict they might become.

The U.S. Constitution prohibits the making of *ex post facto* laws.[7] The seminal case construing this constitutional prohibition is *Calder v. Bull.*[8] In *Calder*, the court held that four types of criminal laws were unconstitutional because they were *ex post facto*.[9] These four were as follows:

> 1st. Every law that makes an action done before the passing of the law, and which was innocent when done, criminal; and punishes such action. 2d. Every law that aggravates a crime, or makes it greater than it was when committed. 3d. Every law that changes the punishment, and inflicts a greater punishment, than the law annexed to the crime, when committed. 4th. Every law that alters the legal rules of evidence, and receives less, or different, testimony, than the law required at the time of the commission of the offense, in order to convict the offender.[10]

Also note that, although there are certain instances when *civil* laws will be allowed to operate retrospectively, those instances generally occur when the legislature passes remedial or curative statutes.[11] Nevertheless, those retrospective laws are civil not criminal.

HABEAS CORPUS

The phrase *habeas corpus* means "you may retain the body."[12]

The term *habeas corpus* typically refers to a writ of *habeas corpus*. The United States Constitution provides that, "[t]he privilege of the

Writ of Habeas Corpus shall not be suspended, unless when in Cases of Rebellion or Invasion the public Safety may require it."[13]

The "body" (*corpus*) at issue in a writ of *habeas corpus* is the body of a prisoner. Historically, a prisoner employed a writ of *habeas corpus* in an attempt to challenge his/her detention after being convicted. Today prisoners may attempt to use *habeas* proceedings even in an effort to be released from detention before trial.

Nevertheless, the typical writ of *habeas corpus* scenario is as follows. A criminal suspect is tried and convicted in a state court on criminal charges. The prisoner is then incarcerated. The prisoner next brings a writ of *habeas corpus* to a federal court asking that court to review the state conviction *de novo*[14] in order to determine whether the state conviction itself or the manner in which s/he was convicted violated the prisoner's constitutional rights.

One of the most famous cases which arose from a *habeas corpus* petition is *Gideon v. Wainwright*.[15] In *Gideon*, the prisoner, Clarence Gideon, was imprisoned in Florida after having been convicted of "having broken and entered a poolroom with intent to commit a misdemeanor."[16] However, at his trial the state of Florida had refused to provide him with a lawyer for his defense. The U.S. Supreme Court held that, because the sixth amendment guarantees that the accused in all criminal prosecutions "shall enjoy the right . . . to have the assistance of counsel for his defense," Gideon's conviction was unconstitutional.[17] Gideon's writ of *habeas corpus* was the vehicle that permitted him to bring his case to the U.S. Supreme Court in the first place. In essence the writ said "Mr. Sheriff, you may retain Mr. Gideon's body so that the U.S. Supreme Court can decide his case."[18]

The federal statutory authority for *habeas corpus* today is found in 28 U.S. Code §§ 2241-2255. In short, these Code sections afford a prisoner the opportunity to have a federal court review the constitutionality of his/her incarceration by either a state or federal court resulting from a criminal conviction.

MENS REA

Mens rea means "an evil mind."[19] As was observed above, crimes generally involve both physical (objective) and mental (subjective) components.[20] The term *mens rea* actually derives from the complete

Latin expression, *actus non facit reum nisi mens sit rea* ("an act [by itself] does not make a person guilty unless the mind is evil").[21]

A person must possess a *mens rea* as a condition precedent to being criminally liable for a given crime. This is the reason why someone who is insane cannot be criminally liable for his/her actions. An insane person is said to be incapable of possessing "an evil mind" because s/he cannot comprehend the significance of his/her conduct.[22] However, it is dangerous to generalize about the concept of *mens rea* because different crimes require different degrees of mental awareness.

Some crimes require that the actor's conduct be intentional before culpability arises. Others require that a person merely have knowledge of the nature of his/her act or the consequences of that act. Still other crimes arise only when a person realizes that his/her conduct is creating significant risks to others (i.e., reckless conduct). Finally, sometimes a person need only be grossly negligent (i.e., not even fully aware of the risk to others) in order to be deemed to possess a culpable state of mind.

Therefore, since there is no universal state of mind which constitutes the requisite *mens rea* for all crimes, law students and lawyers must be sensitive to the state of mind required for whatever particular crime it is which they are studying or researching.[23]

NOLLE PROSEQUI

Nolle prosequi means "to wish not to pursue."[24]

In the context of criminal law, it is the state district attorney or federal prosecutor who most often uses the device of *nolle prosequi*. In certain types of cases the district attorney simply determines that a case is not worth full litigation. Or the prosecutor may decide that certain charges (i.e., not the entire case) are not worth full litigation. In such cases, the prosecutor enters "nolle" (the commonly accepted shorthand for the phrase *nolle prosequi*) on the record, indicating that s/he does not wish to prosecute.

Under what circumstances does a prosecutor decide to "nolle" a case? If a prosecutor is convinced that there is insufficient evidence to convict a defendant, s/he may not wish to pursue the case. If witnesses either fail to testify or refuse to appear, a prosecutor may *nolle* a case (lest the court dismiss the case for good).[25] In general

---

a prosecutor is most likely to *nolle* a case when the charges are relatively insubstantial and the evidence thin.[26]

Clearly, a prosecutor's decision whether to *nolle* a case involves broad discretion. Consequently, a number of jurisdictions have created legislation or court rules that require a prosecutor either to explain his/her reasons for nolleing a case in writing or to obtain court approval prior to entering *nolle* in a case.[27]

NOLO CONTENDERE

The phrase *nolo contendere* means "I do not want to contest."[28]

Laypersons generally assume that a defendant can either plead "innocent" or "guilty." However, in addition, a criminal defendant can also attempt to plead *nolo contendere*. A plea of *nolo contendere* is more similar to a plea of "guilty" than to a plea of "innocent." Nevertheless there are important factors which distinguish a plea of *nolo contendere* from a "guilty" plea. First, before a defendant in a federal case can enter a plea of *nolo contendere*, the court must grant permission to do so.[29] Furthermore, unlike a "guilty" plea, a plea of *nolo contendere* does not indicate that the defendant admits the charges. Nevertheless, a court typically imposes some sort of criminal sanctions (e.g., fines or incarceration) as a result of a plea of *nolo contendere*. Finally, unlike a "guilty" plea, which may be used against a defendant in a subsequent civil suit, a plea of *nolo contendere* cannot be so used.[30]

Commentators have criticized the continued acceptance of the *nolo contendere* plea but most also recognize its utility. For example, shortly after the state of Nebraska made a plea of *nolo contendere* available in 1953, a student note in the Nebraska Law Review examined the issue:

> Whether the plea of *nolo contendere* serves any useful function in a system of state criminal procedure is a debatable question. Several states have eliminated the plea from their practice, and the court of another state in which the plea is used has questioned its desirability in modern practice. The American Law Institute's Code of Criminal Procedure expressly abolishes all pleas other than guilty or not guilty, and England, in which the plea had its origin and early development, has long since dispensed with its

use. On the other hand, the non-admissibility of the plea in collateral civil proceedings may often be a characteristic which will induce a defendant, who would otherwise plead not guilty and undergo a trial rather than provide an admission usable by his expected adversary in a subsequent civil action, to save both his time and that of the prosecuting authorities by entering a *nolo* plea.[31]

■ ENDNOTES

1. *Actus* is a Latin noun meaning, here, "an action" or "a deed." *Reus* is used in this phrase as an adjective meaning "evil" or "guilty."
2. J. Hall, General Principles of Criminal Law 223 (1947).
3. *See*, e.g., LaFave and Scott, Substantive Criminal Law § 3.2 (1986).
4. *See Mens Rea, infra.*
5. Saunders, *Voluntary Acts and the Criminal Law*, 49 U. Pitt. L. Rev. 443, 452 (1988).
6. In Latin the preposition *ex* means "from" or "out of." *Post* simply means "after." *Facto* is the perfect passive participle of the Latin verb *facere* ("to make" or "to do") and thus means "that which was done" or "a deed."
7. U.S. Const. art. I, §§ 9 & 10.
8. 3 Dall. 386 (1798).
9. *Id.* at 390.
10. *Id.*
11. *See* 73 Am. Jur. 2d, *Statutes*, §§ 353-54 (1985).
12. The verb *habeas* is the second-person singular present subjunctive (here a hortatory subjunctive) of the verb *habēre* ("to have, to hold, to retain, to keep, etc."). As such, it means "you may retain." *Corpus* is the accusative singular of the noun *corpus* ("body"). The original phrase from which we get *habeas corpus* was *habeas corpus ad subjiciendum* ("you may retain the body of the prisoner for the purpose of subjecting him to the authority of a magistrate"). Thus the subject of the verb *habeas* (the "you") is the sheriff or other official of the state who has control over the prisoner's person.
13. U.S. Const. art. I, § 9.
14. *See* discussion of the phrase *De Novo* in General Terms, *infra.*
15. 372 U.S. 335 (1963).
16. *Id.* at 336.
17. *Id.* at 345.

18. Other constitutional violations can bring about a prisoner's petition for writ of *habeas corpus* as well. S/he may argue that the trial court lacked proper jurisdiction. S/he may, in fact, argue that any number of constitutional irregularities tainted the conviction. Therefore, technically, no criminal conviction is final until all petitions for *habeas corpus* have been rejected by the federal courts.

19. The Latin noun *mens* means "mind." *Rea*, here, is the adjective "evil, wrongful, guilty" (*rea* is simply the feminine form of the same adjective which appears above in the phrase *actus reus*). Because the phrase *mens rea* is vital to the study of criminal law, I must caution students that a comprehensive discussion of this complex concept is simply beyond the scope of this book. What I intend to provide is merely a thumbnail sketch suitable to provide a general understanding of *mens rea*. Students should consult hornbooks, treatises, encyclopedias, and law review articles specifically designed for criminal law in order to find more comprehensive discussions of the phrase *mens rea*.

20. *See Actus Reus, supra.*

21. *See generally* LaFave and Scott, *supra* note 3, at § 3.4 (1986).

22. *See M'Naughten's Case*, 8 Eng. Rep. 718 (1843) and LaFave and Scott, *supra* note 3, at § 4.2 (1986).

23. Under the Model Penal Code, the four most common degrees of *mens rea* are intent, knowledge, recklessness, and negligence. The Model Penal Code defines these different degrees of *mens rea* as follows:

(2) Kinds of Culpability Defined.

(a) Purposely.
   A person acts purposely with respect to a material element of an offense when:
   (i) if the element involves the nature of his conduct or a result thereof, it is his conscious object to engage in conduct of that nature or to cause such a result; and
   (ii) if the element involves the attendant circumstances, he is aware of the existence of such circumstances or he believes or hopes that they exist.

(b) Knowingly.
   A person acts knowingly with respect to a material element of an offense when:
   (i) if the element involves the nature of his conduct or the attendant circumstances, he is aware that his conduct is of that nature or that such circumstances exist; and
   (ii) if the element involves a result of his conduct, he is aware that it is practically certain that his conduct will cause such a result.

(c) Recklessly.
   A person acts recklessly with respect to a material element of an

offense when he consciously disregards a substantial and unjustifiable risk that the material element exists or will result from his conduct. The risk must be of such a nature and degree that, considering the nature and purpose of the actor's conduct and the circumstances known to him, its disregard involves a gross deviation from the standard of conduct that a law-abiding person would observe in the actor's situation.

(d) Negligently.

A person acts negligently with respect to a material element of an offense when he should be aware of a substantial and unjustifiable risk that the material element exists or will result from his conduct. The risk must be of such a nature and degree that the actor's failure to perceive it, considering the nature and purpose of his conduct and the circumstances known to him, involves a gross deviation from the standard of care that a reasonable person would observe in the actor's situation.

Model Penal Code § 2.02(2) (1962).

24. *Nolle* is the present active infinitive of the verb *nolle* ("to be unwilling, to not wish, to not want"). *Prosequi* is the present infinitive of the deponent verb *prosequi* ("to follow" or "to attack, pursue").

25. Prosecutors sometimes enter *nolle prosequi* (or simply "nolle") on the record in cases involving shoplifting (this is especially true when the shoplifter is a first-time offender who has been sufficiently frightened by the arrest itself).

26. Another Latin phrase often bounced around in the legal profession which is relevant here is *de minimis non curat lex* ("the law is not concerned about trivial matters").

27. *See* W. LaFave and A. Scott, Criminal Procedure § 13.3(c) 181-182 (1984).

28. In Latin the verb *nolo* is the first-person singular present active form of the verb *nolle* ("to be unwilling" or "to not want"—the same verb which appears in the phrase *nolle prosequi, supra*). As such, *nolo* means "I do not want." *Contendere* is the present active infinitive of *contendere* ("to strain, exert" or "to strive with another"). It is clear that in this phrase the word *contendere* has taken on its more modern meaning "to contend" or "to contest."

29. Fed. R. Crim. P. 11 (b) provides that "a defendant may plead nolo contendere only with the consent of the court. Such a plea shall be accepted by the court only after due consideration of the views of the parties and the interest of the public in the effective administration of justice." Fed. R. Civ. P. 11 (c) requires that a defendant must understand the import of what a plea of *nolo contendere* entails.

30. *See,* e.g., Fed. R. Evid. 410.

CHAPTER SIX

EVIDENCE

■ THE ROMAN BACKGROUND

During the Roman Republic there were few, if any, formal, codified rules of evidence. The *judex* ("judge") had wide latitude as to what he might consider relevant or probative. Judges admitted hearsay evidence but apparently afforded it less weight than a witness's live testimony. Each party bore the responsibility of securing his own witnesses. There was no such thing as a court subpoena to compel a witness to appear in court. The judges did not permit either the parties or their close relatives to testify as witnesses at trial. As a general rule, a party who asserted a fact had the burden of proving it. A plaintiff ordinarily had the burden of proving his case but a defendant was required to bear the burden of proving an affirmative defense if he asserted one. The judges recognized some presumptions, both rebuttable and conclusive.

When the Roman Empire was in full swing, the rules of evidence evolved into a detailed and somewhat rigid road map for advocates. Judges in the Empire preferred documentary evidence to the testimony of witnesses. The Emperor Constantine (c. 300 A.D.) introduced the rule of *testis unus, testis nullus* ("one witness, no witness"). This rule of evidence provided that the testimony of one witness was worthless unless corroborated by another. Witnesses who were absent could, nevertheless, write statements which could be introduced into evidence. Judges endeavored to exclude hearsay testimony and it was the judges who asked witnesses questions. There were also complicated rules that governed the introduction of documents at trial.

The Roman rules, however, never attained the degree of detail and scope of our modern state and federal rules of evidence. The cornerstone of our present-day rules of evidence is the concept of relevance. Testimony, documents and material objects are admissible into evidence at trial only if they are relevant to the issues presented in the case. Our system of admitting and excluding matter offered as evidence strives to ensure that the jury only considers those things which are pertinent and reliable. Constitutional law also influences our rules of evidence, primarily because an accused is constitutionally entitled to confront (i.e., cross-examine) witnesses who testify against him/her. Law students usually concentrate on the Federal Rules of Evidence and topics such as relevance, materiality, documents, direct and cross-examination, and hearsay.

CRIMEN FALSI

Crimen falsi translates into English as "a crime of falsehood."[1] When a litigator cross-examines a witness at trial, s/he commonly tries to cast doubt on that person's testimony by trying to convince the jury not to believe what the witness has said during direct questioning by the opposing counsel. Litigators attempt to cast doubt on the credibility of a witness through a variety of techniques of impeachment. The trial attorney might try to show that the witness is biased (i.e., that s/he has some personal interest in the outcome of the case—perhaps the witness is a close friend of one of the parties or has a strong emotional attachment to the cause of one of the parties) and therefore cannot be trusted. Lawyers also may attempt to catch the witness saying something that directly conflicts or contradicts what s/he had said earlier (the so-called prior inconsistent statement).[2] Lawyers also often try either to prove or suggest that the witness was unable to see accurately or hear clearly the event about which they testified (e.g., counsel might try to show that the witness's view was obstructed or perhaps that the witness was not wearing the glasses that s/he usually wears, etc.). Another method of impeaching a witness is to show the jury that the person on the stand is the type of person likely to tell lies. The Federal Rules of Evidence provide that an attorney may attack a witness's credibility by "evidence that the witness has been convicted of a crime . . . but only if the crime . . . involved dishonesty or false statement. . . . "[3] The rule also requires that evidence of such a crime of falsehood must come directly from the witness's testimony or by introducing some public record of the crime during cross-examination.[4] This rule regarding the introduction of evidence of a *crimen falsi*, for purposes of impeachment, is a vestige of the old common law precept that a person's conviction of either a felony or a *crimen falsi* automatically rendered that individual incompetent to testify as a witness.[5] Today some jurisdictions distinguish between crimes that are classified as felonies and those that are classified as misdemeanors.[6] However, most states' rules of evidence permit impeachment using a misdemeanor "if the illegal act involved dishonesty or a false statement"[7] Thus, as a general rule, most jurisdictions endorse the use of convictions for *crimen falsi* to impeach a witness's testimony, without regard to whether that crime was a felony or merely a misdemeanor.

But what are these "crimes of falsehood" that a trial lawyer can employ to discredit a witness? Obviously perjury—giving false testimony—is the paradigmatic example of a *crimen falsi*. Mail fraud, forgery, bribery, and tax evasion are other crimes that clearly involve falsehood, deceit, or dishonesty.[8] Courts have, however, held that other crimes that ostensibly have little to do with dishonesty except that they are crimes (and, therefore, inherently evince dishonesty) may also fall under the rubric of *crimen falsi*.[9]

FALSUS IN UNO, FALSUS IN OMNIBUS

This maxim means "deceitful/lying in one instance, [therefore] deceitful/lying in all."[10] As was just discussed, when a witness has been convicted of a crime involving "dishonesty or false statement," a lawyer may introduce evidence of that conviction in order to discredit the witness's testimony.[11] The rationale which permits evidence of this nature is rather uncomplicated; if the witness has been caught lying or deceiving on a previous occasion, it is likely that s/he will lie or deceive again. Basically, the lawyer is saying to the jury, "listen people, we caught this witness lying before, what makes you think that s/he isn't lying now?" The best indicator of future conduct is past conduct.

Modern rules of evidence recognize the validity of this logic but typically limit its application to *convictions of crimes* involving dishonesty or falsehood. For example, suppose that the person on the stand has occasionally told lies. In fact, let's assume that the lawyer knows for a fact that on the previous Saturday night when asked about her age the witness said that she was 29 (when in reality she is 33). Let's assume further that the witness's age is entirely irrelevant and unrelated to the merits of the case or anything involved in her testimony. Should we allow the lawyer to introduce evidence (say a tape recording) of her lying about her age so that s/he (the lawyer) can then show the jury that she had lied about her age? The attorney's sole purpose for wanting to prove that the witness lied is so that s/he can then argue *falsus in uno, falsus in omnibus* to the jury.

The Federal Rules of Evidence do make it possible for attorneys to lay the groundwork for a *falsus in uno* argument, but as a practical matter courts seldom permit such evidence.[12] Rule 608 provides that an attorney may impeach a witness's credibility by evidence of "specific instances of conduct" (e.g., specific lies told by the witness) even when the particular act is not a crime covered by Rule 609.[13] However, such evidence is only admissible under the following circumstances: (1) when introduced during cross-examination; (2) when the specific instance sought to be introduced is "probative of truthfulness or untruthfulness . . . concerning the witness' character for truthfulness or untruthfulness, or . . . concerning the character for truthfulness or untruthfulness of another witness as to which character the witness being cross examined has testified"; and (3) when the court, in its discretion, decides to allow it.[14]

Similarly, if an attorney desires to show that a witness has a reputation for lying (and thus wants to launch a *falsus in uno* attack based upon the witness's reputation for lying), the Federal Rules make it technically possible to introduce such evidence of reputation as well.[15] Rule 608(a) permits impeachment "in the form of opinion or reputation only when the evidence refers to the witness's character for truthfulness or untruthfulness.[16] Nevertheless, courts have been extremely reluctant to permit extrinsic evidence to show that in the past a witness has lied about collateral matters (i.e., matters unrelated to the litigation).[17] "On balance, they have held that consideration of time and distraction militate against production of additional evidence on factual propositions which have no direct or circumstantial bearing on any element of a claim or defense."[18] As a general rule, there are plenty of more effective ways to discredit a witness's testimony than to pursue a *falsus in uno, falsus in omnibus* argument. Thus, the *falsus in uno* concept is viable to the extent that the maxim applies to *crimen falsi* (e.g., as interpreted under Fed. R. Evid. 609(a)(2)), but to the extent that attorneys attempt to use it to introduce extrinsic evidence of a mendacious reputation or even particular instances of lying (when such matters are collateral), modern American evidentiary rules have tended to reject the doctrine.

IN LIMINE

In limine means "on the doorstep" or "in the threshold/entrance/doorway."[19] In the law of evidence, this phrase relates to motions *in limine.*

Litigators file a host of pretrial motions. In fact, most litigators spend far more time writing pretrial motions than they do arguing in a court. Nevertheless, even though many motions are filed prior to trial, not all of these are called motions *in limine*. Technically speaking, a motion *in limine* is a pretrial motion by which a lawyer attempts to prevent opposing counsel from introducing certain evidence or certain kinds of evidence at trial. Traditionally, lawyers have used motions *in limine* to exclude matters, facts, documents, etc. that would contravene the rules of evidence if admitted.[20]

Professor McCormick characterizes the purpose of motions *in limine* as an attorney's effort either to insulate the jury from potentially "harmful inadmissible evidence" or to secure a strategic advantage.[21]

Although there may have once existed a technical distinction between a motion *in limine* (i.e., to exclude evidence that might conflict with "some ordinary rule of evidence") as opposed to a pretrial motion to suppress evidence that was violative of the party's constitutional rights, as a practical matter today the bench and bar ordinarily refer to both types of pretrial motions to exclude or suppress improper evidence as motions *in limine.*[22] The Federal Rules of Criminal Procedure state that parties must raise "motions to suppress evidence" before trial.[23] This practice has long been common, especially in criminal trials, and courts have begun recognizing the utility of *in limine* motions in civil cases as well.[24]

Most rules governing *in limine* motions grant the trial judge broad discretion regarding whether to rule quickly or instead to take more of a wait-and-see approach on the motion.[25] However, given the nature of evidentiary motions *in limine*, judges typically prefer to rule in a timely fashion in order to allow the parties the opportunity to plan their trial strategy accordingly.[26] However, technically speaking, a judge's ruling on a motion *in limine* is not considered a final ruling on the issue.[27] Therefore, courts have had to wrestle with whether a judge's ruling *in limine* is subject to review by an appellate court, where the party fails to object at trial. The authority is split on this issue but the outcome may depend, at least in part, on the language of the judge's ruling on the motion.[28]

PRIMA FACIE

The phrase *prima facie* in a legal context means "with the first outward appearance."[29] In all civil law cases, a plaintiff is required to present a *prima facie* case against the defendant. If s/he does not, the defendant automatically prevails.

Every cause of action has certain basic elements which a plaintiff must allege and prove in order to prevail. A plaintiff presents a *prima facie* case by alleging and offering proof of each of those elements. In other words, by alleging and offering proof of those basic elements which constitute his/her particular cause of action, the plaintiff in one sense "wins" with the first outward appearance of the case. By presenting a *prima facie* case against the defendant, the plaintiff smashes the ball squarely into the defendant's court. If the defendant is unable to establish some sort of excuse or affirmative defense after the plaintiff has established a *prima facie* case, in the absence of highly unusual circumstances, the plaintiff will prevail.

In litigation the plaintiff has the initial burden of proof. Another way of expressing essentially the same idea is to say that the plaintiff must establish a *prima facie* case. After the plaintiff has established a *prima facie* case, the burden of proof is said to "shift" to the defendant. Thereafter, the defendant must prove excuse or an affirmative defense, or else lose.

For example, torts classes in law school study the concept of negligence.[30] In order for a plaintiff to establish a *prima facie* case of negligence, s/he must prove four essential elements. S/he must prove that the defendant had legal duty which was owed to the plaintiff (e.g., a lifeguard has a duty to avoid unreasonable risk to the swimmers under his/her supervision). S/he must prove that the defendant breached that duty which was owed (e.g., the lifeguard was kissing his/her girl/boyfriend behind the boathouse instead of supervising the beachfront). S/he must prove that the defendant's breach of duty to the plaintiff was the proximate or legal cause of the injury to the plaintiff.[31] Finally, the plaintiff must prove that s/he has actually suffered an injury (e.g., a specialist might testify concerning the extent of brain damage due to loss of oxygen when the plaintiff went under). If the plaintiff fails to establish a *prima facie* case of negligence by failing to prove any of these four elements, s/he cannot prevail. If, on the other hand, s/he does establish a *prima facie* case of negligence, the defendant has the burden of proving some excuse or affirmative defense in order to escape liability for the plaintiff's injury.

The term *prima facie* also occurs in an evidentiary context when lawyers refer to documents that are *"prima facie* genuine."[32] Generally, when litigators introduce documents into evidence, they are required to show that the documents offered are, in fact, authentic.[33] Most rules of evidence provide a variety of techniques for proving that a document is authentic. For example, a witness who actually saw a document prepared or signed can testify regarding its authenticity. It is also common practice to use testimony to show the chain of custody of a document.[34] However, modern evidentiary rules and statutes also recognize that certain documents are so likely to be authentic that they are considered *prima facie* genuine, or "self-authenticating."[35] Such "self-authenticating" documents may be introduced as evidence without the need to offer other extrinsic evidence of authenticity. The Federal Rules provide that a number of types of documents are self-authenticating, such as documents bearing a governmental seal; certified copies of documents; and official books, pamphlets, and other publications issued by public authority.[36] Thus, for example, if you were litigating a case involving trademark infringement and you wanted to prove that your client owned a trademark that had been duly registered in the U.S. Patent and Trademark Office, you could introduce the official registration certificate itself, since it bears the commissioner's seal; you could introduce a certified copy of the registration certificate issued by the Trademark Office; and you could also introduce a copy of the *Official Gazette*, the official weekly publication of the U.S. Patent and Trademark Office, which publishes, among other things, a list of registration certificates issued. All three forms of evidence would be *prima facie* genuine under the Federal Rules.[37] The Federal Rules also characterize newspapers, periodicals, checks, promissory notes, and tags, labels, or inscriptions that indicate the "ownership, control or origin" of goods or services as "self-authenticating."[38] However, merely because a document is *prima facie* genuine does not necessarily mean that it is, in fact, authentic and that its authenticity cannot be challenged. It simply means that "on first appearance" the document appears genuine. Consequently, the party wishing to introduce it need not provide extrinsic evidence to prove authenticity. Opposing counsel may still freely attempt to show that the document, although apparently valid on its face, is a fraud, fake, forgery, or is otherwise unreliable.

QUI TACET CONSENTIRE VIDETUR, UBI TRACTATUR DE EJUS COMMODO

This Latin maxim expresses a notion that has generated a great deal of debate: "[s/he] who says nothing appears to agree deliberately, when that which is being discussed concerns his/her interest."[39]

This somewhat cryptic maxim expresses the belief that a person can admit facts and other things by silence. We customarily assume that when confronted with a false accusation, human nature will spark us to deny it. The logical extrapolation of the notion that humans instinctively deny false accusations is the notion that failure to do so is an admission of that accusation. Modern laws of evidence generally endorse the presumption of *qui tacet consentire videtur*, but the state and federal limitations on its application can be complicated and, in many instances, subject to interpretation.

An admission is strong evidence. When someone simply admits having done or said something, the judicial system is spared the rigor of proving the fact by witnesses, objects, documents, or circumstantial evidence. Even though Perry Mason was able to pull it off on a weekly basis, in real life witnesses rarely fall apart under oath and admit arson, rape, burglary, murder, etc. Sorry, Perry.

Law students ordinarily deal with admissions in their evidence class when studying hearsay. Clearly, a detailed discussion of "hearsay" is well beyond the scope of this book. The Federal Rules of Evidence articulate what is probably the most well known and widely accepted definition: " 'Hearsay' is a statement, other than one made by the declarant while testifying at the trial or hearing, offered in evidence to prove the truth of the matter asserted."[40] However, the Federal Rules expressly define certain admissions, which can be admissions by silence, as not hearsay; and characterize other forms of admissions, even admissions by silence, as exceptions to hearsay (and consequently admissible).[41]

Nevertheless, even though the Federal Rules permit the introduction of an admission by silence, courts have recognized that an accused's *Miranda* rights and other logical limitations must be considered when determining the reliability of an admission by silence.[42] Professor McCormick has noted that courts must take into account certain fundamental considerations; for example, the party who is claimed to have made an admission must have actually heard the statement which s/he is supposed to have admitted; the party must have understood the statement; the party must have known the subject matter of the statement (i.e., why would someone deny an act that s/he did not even know had been done?); the party cannot suffer from physical or emotional handicaps that would prevent a denial; and, of course, "[p]robably most important of all, the statement itself must be such as would, if untrue, call for a denial under the circumstances."[43] Professor McCormick has articulated the basic test as follows: "whether a reasonable person would have denied under the circumstances, with answers not lending themselves readily to mechanical formulations."[44]

Thus, the second portion of the Latin maxim, *ubi tractatur de ejus commodo*, is highly significant. Silence alone does not constitute an admission. Rather, one must apply constitutional principles, rules of hearsay evidence, and logic in order to deal with a question of tacit admission properly.

RES GESTAE

Most Latin students or students of Roman history are rarely confused by this phrase; they know that the phrase *res gestae* means "things that have been done."[45] Law students, on the other hand, and lawyers and judges too, are more often perplexed than enlightened by it. There is good reason for this confusion too. Professor Morgan remarked, "The marvelous capacity of a Latin phrase to serve as a substitute for reasoning, and the confusion of thought inevitably accompanying the use of inaccurate terminology, are nowhere better illustrated than in the decisions dealing with the admissibility of evidence as 'res gestae.' "[46]

As was noted above, modern rules of evidence ordinarily prohibit hearsay evidence unless it falls within the scope of some hearsay exception.[47] In the nineteenth century, before Anglo-American jurisprudence had articulated the myriad rules of hearsay that have now evolved, courts seeking to establish those rules formulated the principle that certain statements which had been made spontaneously and roughly contemporaneously with the act in question at trial were admissible because they were part of the *res gestae*.[48]

Modern rules of evidence classify statements that courts once classified under the rubric of *res gestae* (thereby avoiding the prohibition against hearsay) either as hearsay exceptions or not hearsay at all.[49] The phrase *res gestae* does not appear anywhere in the Federal Rules of Evidence. However, judges and lawyers still use the term and often fail to pinpoint the modern categorization; instead they haphazardly refer to hearsay exceptions as *res gestae* rather than "present sense impressions,"[50] statements concerning the declarant's physical condition,[51] so-called "excited utterances,"[52] or statements regarding present mental or emotional state.[53]

Clearly statements that can be called *res gestae* all tend to involve spontaneity.[54] Our common sense tells us that when people blurt out statements without giving themselves time to reflect, and thereby time to fabricate, such statements are more likely to be credible than not. And, since the hearsay rule is designed, at least in part, to ensure that only truthful statements reach the ears of the jury, to the extent that statements made as part of the *res gestae* are spontaneous, it is logical that they should be admissible.

Professor McCormick emphasizes that the vague nature of the notion "made it easier for courts to broaden its coverage and thus provide for the admissibility of certain statements in new situations."[55] Nevertheless, McCormick's praise is part of his eulogy for the term, for he concludes that "the law has now reached a stage at which widening admissibility will be best served by other means. The ancient phrase can well be jettisoned, with due acknowledgement that it served its era in the evolution of evidence law."[56] Obviously, as a practical matter, a law student faced with *res gestae* as a possible answer on a multiple choice test in evidence would be well advised to steer clear. By the same token, it is hard to imagine that any self-respecting trial attorney could tell the judge with a straight face that his/her evidence was admissible as a hearsay exception because it was part of the *res gestae*.[57]

■ ENDNOTES

1. *Crimen* is a noun meaning "indictment, charge, accusation, misdeed, crime." *Falsi* is the genitive singular of the noun *falsum*, "an untruth, falsehood, lie, misstatement, untrue representation." Here *falsi* is a genitive of description and may be rendered simply as "of falsehood."

2. *See* Fed. R. Evid. 613(b).

3. Fed. R. Evid. 609(a)(2). Rule 609(a)(1) provides that evidence of a crime may also be admitted where the crime "was punishable by death or imprisonment in excess of one year . . . and the court determines that the probative value of admitting this evidence outweighs its prejudicial effect to the defendant. . . ."

4. *Id.*

5. E. Cleary, McCormick on Evidence, § 43 at 93 (3d ed. 1984).

6. G. Lilly, An Introduction to the Law of Evidence § 8.3 at 344 (2d ed. 1987).

7. *Id.*

8. *Id.* at 348-49. Professor Wigmore noted that "the extent and meaning of the term, 'crimen falsi,' in our law is nowhere laid down with precision. In Roman law, from which we have borrowed the term, it included not only forgery, but every species of fraud and deceit." 3 J. Wigmore, Evidence § 520 at 730 (1970).

9. *See*, e.g., *United States v. Carden*, 529 F.2d 433 (5th Cir. 1976), cert. denied, 429 U.S. 848 (holding that the witness's prior conviction for petty larceny was admissible as a crime that "involved his honesty or false statement" under Fed. R. Evid. 609(a)(2).

10. *Falsus* here is an adjective meaning "false, lying, mendacious, misleading, deceptive." *Uno* is the ablative singular of the cardinal numeral *unus* ("one") and *omnibus* is the ablative plural of the noun *omnis* (which means "each" or "every" in the singular and "all" in the plural). Both *uno* and *omnibus* are objects of the preposition, *in*, which simply means "in."

11. *See Crimen Falsi, supra.*

12. G. Lilly, *supra* note 6 § 8.6 at 368.

13. Fed. R. Evid. 608(b).

14. *Id.*

15. Fed. R. Evid. 608(a).

16. *Id.*

17. G. Lilly, *supra* note 6 § 8.6 at 368. *See also* Wigmore, *supra* note 8 at §§ 1008-15 (1970).

18. *Id.*

19. *In* is a preposition that simply means "in" or "on." *Limine* is the ablative singular form of the noun *limen* ("doorstep, threshold, entrance, the point at which something passes into something").

20. E. Cleary, *supra* note 5, § 180 at 521 n. 10.

21. *Id.* at 128. *See also* J. Wigmore *supra* note 8, § 18 n. 7.

22. *Dep't of Pub. Works and Bldg's v. Roehrig*, 45 Ill. App. 3d, 359 N.E. 2d (1976); G. Lilly, *supra* note 6 at 480.

23. Fed. R. Crim. P. 12(b)(3).

24. G. Lilly, *supra* note 6 at 481.

25. For example, the Federal Rules of Criminal Procedure require that the judge rule on all pretrial motions to suppress evidence "unless the court, for good cause, orders that [the motion] be deferred for determination at the trial of the general issue or until after verdict." Fed. R. Crim. P. 12(e).

26. E. Cleary, *supra* note 5, § 180 at 523; G. Lilly, *supra* note 6 at 481.

27. Lilly, *supra* note 6 at 481.

28. *Id.* Citing *Hale v. Firestone Tire & Rubber Co.*, 756 F.2d 1322, 1333 (8th Cir. 1985) for the proposition that "a motion in limine does not preserve error for appellate review," and *Sprynczynatyk v. General Motors Corp.*, 771 F.2d 1112 (8th Cir. 1985), cert. denied, 106 S. Ct. 1263 (1986) for the proposition that an objection at trial is unnecessary to preserve the issue for appeal when the judge's ruling is clearly definitive.

29. In Latin the adjective *prima* is the ordinal numeral which means "first." The noun *facies* has several meanings, such as "shape, form, figure," or even generally "outward appearance, face, countenance, character, nature." Both words in this phrase are in the ablative case and are together an example of the Latin construction called an ablative of means. An ablative of means is generally translated with the words "by," "by means of," or "with."

30. At the risk of using a Latin phrase which I will assume is self-explanatory, law students probably study the concept of negligence *ad nauseam*.

31. Proximate cause is one of the slipperiest concepts in all of tort law (suffice it to say that it is clear that the plaintiff, in our lifeguard hypothetical, would not have suffered severe brain damage from almost drowning if the lifeguard had been performing his/her duties as any reasonable lifeguard in a similar situation would have).

32. G. Lilly, *supra* note 6, at 528.

33. Fed. R. Evid. 901.

34. *See generally* Gianelli, *Chain of Custody and the Handling of Real Evidence*, 20 Am. Crim. L. Rev. 527 (1983). *See also* E. Cleary, *supra* note 5, § 219, at 687-88 and § 224, at 694-95.

35. G. Lilly, *supra,* note 6, § 13. At 527-28.

36. Fed. R. Evid. 902(1),(4),(5).

37. *Id.*

38. Fed. R. Evid. 902(6),(7),(9).

39. *Qui* is the nominative singular form of the relative pronoun ("who"), and is the subject of the verb *tacet,* which is third-person singular present tense indicative of *tacere* ("to be silent"). Thus, *qui tacet* means "s/he who is silent." *Videtur* is the third-person singular present passive indicative of *videre* ("to see"), which in the passive voice is normally translated "to seem" or "to appear." *Videtur,* then, means "s/he appears." *Consentire* is the present active infinitive of *consentire* ("to be in harmony or unison in opinion" or "to be in agreement, to concur"). *Ubi* means "when." *Tractatur* is the third-person singular present passive form of *tractare* ("to keep pulling or dragging" or "to deal with, to examine, discuss, or consider"). Hence, *tractatur* here means something on the order of "it is being discussed" or "it is being considered." *De* is a preposition meaning "about" or "concerning." *Commodo* is the object of the preposition *de. Commodo* is the ablative singular of *commodum* ("an advantage, benefit" or "interest, profit, convenience"). *Eius* is both the masculine and feminine genitive singular of the demonstrative pronoun *is ea, id* ("he, she, it") and thus means "his" or "her." Therefore, the phrase *de ejus commodo* means "concerning his/her interest."

40. Fed. R. Evid. 801(c). Rules 801(a) and 801(b) define the terms "statement" and "declarant" as follows: "A 'statement' is (1) an oral or written assertion or (2) non-verbal conduct of a person, if it is intended by the person as an assertion." "A 'declarant' is a person who makes a statement." *Also see generally* E. Cleary, *supra* note 5, § 246 at 729-30.

41. Fed. R. Evid. 801(d)(2)(B) provides that a statement is not hearsay where "the statement is offered against a party and is . . . a statement of which the party has manifested an adoption or belief in its truth. . . . " Similarly, Fed. R. Evid. 804(b)(3) characterizes as a hearsay exception a statement "if the declarant is unavailable as a witness," "which was at the time of its making so far contrary to the declarant's pecuniary or proprietary interest, or so far tended to subject the declarant to civil or criminal liability, or to render invalid a claim by the declarant against another, that a reasonable person in the declarant's position would not have made the statement unless believing it to be true."

42. E. Cleary, *supra* note 5, § 270 at 800-801. *See also* Gamble, *The Tacit Admission Rule: Unreliable and Unconstitutional,* 14 Ga. L. Rev. 27 (1979).

43. E. Cleary, *supra* note 5, § 270 at 800-801.

44. *Id.*

45. *Res* is the nominative plural of the fifth declension noun *res* ("thing, property, fact, deed, act"), and thus means "things, acts, etc."). *Gestae* is

the perfect passive participle of the third conjugation verb *gerere* ("to hear, carry, perform, transact, do") here in the nominative plural acting as an adjective agreeing with *res*. Ancient Romans used the term *res gestae* to refer to "history." The Emperor Augustus enacted a special monument, the *Res Gestae Divi Augusti*, which narrated in detail the exploits of the Divine Augustus.

46. Morgan, *A Suggested Classification of Utterances Admissible as Res Gestae*, 31 Yale L. J. 229 (1922). *See also* the discussion in Note, *Res Gestae: A Synonym for Confusion*, 20 Baylor L. Rev. 229 (1968).

47. *See* E. Cleary, *supra* note 5, discussion of "hearsay" in *Qui Tacet Consentire Videtur*, *supra*.

48. E. Cleary, *supra* note 5, § 288 at 835. *See generally* J. Wigmore *supra* note 8, § 1767 "History and Meaning of the Phrase Res Gestae."

49. E. Cleary, *supra* note 5, § 288 at 835.

50. Fed. R. Evid. 803(1), "Present Sense Impression," provides that "a statement describing or explaining an event or condition made while the declarant was perceiving the event or condition, or immediately thereafter," is "not excluded by the hearsay rule." For example, statements made by a sportscaster while describing the action of an athletic event could be classified as a "present sense impression" and thus admissible as a hearsay exception.

51. Fed. R. Evid. 803(3), "Then Existing Mental, Emotional, or Physical Condition," provides that "a statement of the declarant's then existing state of mind, emotion, sensation, or physical condition (such as intent, plan, motive, design, mental feeling, pain, and bodily health) . . . " is "not excluded by the hearsay rule." This rule would allow a statement like "I don't know when I've felt better" to be introduced as a hearsay exception. Similarly, Fed. R. Evid. 803(4), "Statement for Purposes of Medical Diagnosis or Treatment," provides that "statements made for purposes of medical diagnosis or treatment and describing medical history, or past or present symptoms, pain, or sensations, or the inception or general character of the cause or external source thereof insofar as reasonably pertinent to diagnosis or treatment" "are not excluded by the hearsay rule." A statement like "Doc, ever since I started playing golf, I've had a shooting pain in my lower back whenever I bend over" would be admissible as a hearsay exception to show, for example, that the declarant's back pain is actually related to his/her golf game and not an automobile accident with the defendant.

52. Fed. R. Evid. 803(2), "Excited Utterance," provides that "a statement relating to a startling event or condition made while the declarant was under the stress of excitement caused by the event or condition" is "not excluded by the hearsay rule." For example, if immediately after a loud explosion aboard an airplane, a passenger heard the pilot scream from the cockpit "My God! I told you not to push that button!", such a statement would probably come under Rule 803(2).

53. Fed. R. Evid. 803(3). *See supra* note 51 and accompanying text. This rule would allow a statement such as "I'm going crazy; the house, the laundry, tax forms, bills, car repair, my job—how the hell do you expect me to cope?" as an exception to the hearsay rule.

54. E. Cleary, *supra* note 5, § 288 at 836. *Also see* J. WIGMORE *supra* note 8, at § 1757.

55. E. Cleary, *supra* note 5, § 288 at 836.

56. *Id.*

57. *Cf.* Lord Blackburn's advice that the way to introduce inadmissible evidence is to "say it is part of the res gestae." Tregarthen, The Law of Hearsay Evidence 21 (1915).

CHAPTER SEVEN

PROPERTY

■ THE ROMAN BACKGROUND

The Roman property laws were among the most systematized, sophisticated, and well developed of all ancient laws. The Romans generally considered property to be anything to which a monetary value could be assigned. Our English word "property" derives from the Latin adjective *proprius* meaning "one's own."

The ancient Romans classified types of property according to a number of characteristics. Among its over half-dozen property classifications, Roman law distinguished between property which was tangible vs. intangible, movable vs. immovable, unique vs. fungible, and divisible vs. indivisible. Many of these classifications are also relevant for property disputes which arise today.

The Romans also distinguished different interests in property. A person could have *proprietas* (or *dominium*) over a *res* ("thing"). *Proprietas* (or *dominium*) constituted what we generally think of as "ownership." The Roman notion of *possessio* was essentially what we call possession. Today we often say that possession is nine points (tenths) of the law (i.e., the rights of a person who possesses property are greater than those of anyone but the true owner; and even the true owner has a heavy burden in order to prove that property possessed by someone else actually belongs to him/her). The ancient Romans were fond of saying *"Beati possidentes"* ("Happy are those who possess") for the same reasons: Roman law recognized the superior claims of those who were in possession of property. In Rome there was also an interest in property called *detentio*. The analogous interest today is bailment. The Latin word *detentio* literally means "a holding aside." In fact, that is exactly what is involved in bailment. For example, if you borrow my lawnmower, it is clear that you do not claim to own it. Instead, you are simply holding it aside for the time being. Similarly, if I ask you to keep my dog for a couple of days while I am out of town, the interest that you take in my dog is also a *detentio*, or bailment. The rights of the parties (e.g., you and I) will vary depending upon the reasons for the *detentio*/bailment. For example, in the case of the lawnmower, you, the bailee, are the one who is intended to benefit. In the case of the dog, it is I, the bailor, who is intended to benefit from the bailment. What is interesting here, I think, is that these concepts (ownership, possession, and bailment) are not new but originated in ancient Roman law.

The Roman methods of acquiring property have influenced modern property law as well. Elements of the earliest, most formulaic, and formalistic method of conveying property (*mancipatio*) can still be seen in our formal transfers of property (e.g., sales of real estate and automobiles). The Roman law of transfer called *traditio* developed some of the basic yet sophisticated concepts relating to the intent of the transferor, the intent of the transferee, and an understanding of what constitutes "delivery" of property from the transferor to the transferee. When law students study the fundamental principles of property early in their first semester, they usually study the Roman concept of *occupatio*. *Occupatio* was the method by which people were deemed to have gained ownership of *res nullius* (things which have never been owned by anyone previously) and other *ferae naturae* (wild animals). The Roman notion of *accessio* provided that a person could acquire the property of another if it, in some way, became inseparably incorporated into property that already belonged to him/her. For example, if someone inadvertently built a house on property which belonged to another, the owner of the principal thing (in this case, the land) became the owner of the house. Finally, the ancient Romans developed a form of adverse possession called *usucapio* (literally "I seize by use").

Roman law also developed various easements and servitudes by which one person could gain limited access to the real property of another. For example, the servitude called *iter* (literally "journey" or "way") allowed a person to walk through property owned by another, the servitude called *actus* ("driven") permitted a person to drive animals over another's land, and the servitude *aquaeductus* ("water drawn") allowed a person to lead or draw water over the land of another person.

As noted above, one of the most salient aspects of Roman property law is the extent to which our notions of property rights and obligations today are either the same as or derived from the ancient Roman laws.

When we think of property laws today, several categories come to mind: personal property, real property, landlord-tenant, and zoning, for example. In law school, students usually focus initially on concepts of estates in land and ownership, and then later consider landlord-tenant, real estate transactions, and zoning. In its broadest sense, property law involves the multitude of rights and responsibilities that arise from the creation, ownership, and transfer of both tangible and intangible property.

CUJUS EST SOLUM EJUS EST USQUE AD COELUM ET USQUE AD INFEROS

"Whose land it is, is his/hers all the way to the sky (Heaven) and all the way to the lower world (Hell)."[1]

This Latin maxim expresses the ancient concept of property law that an owner of real property, in addition to owning the land's surface, also owns the totality of airspace extending above the property without limit and also everything under the surface (presumably all the way down to the center of the earth where the landowner on the opposite side of the globe takes over). In modern jurisprudence the ability to fly has significantly eroded the legal doctrine expressed by this Latin maxim.

The *ad coelum* ("to Heaven") part of the doctrine has been in English law since the days of Lord Coke (pronounced "Cook"), who published an extraordinarily influential four-volume legal treatise in 1628.[2] The earliest American cases which applied the *ad coelum* component of the *cujus est solum* doctrine generally dealt with adjoining landowners. Problems arose when one neighbor built a structure which jutted out in such a way that it was hanging over the other person's property. In these overhanging structures cases, courts generally enforced the property owner's *ad coelum* rights.[3]

Even today courts customarily uphold the *ad coelum* rights of land-owners whose airspace is violated. According to Prosser, "[t]hose who wish to occupy and use the airspace immediately above the surface of land can justifiably be required to pay for the privilege of so doing."[4] Although courts typically are loath to issue injunctions ordering defendants to remove overhanging structures (especially where the cost to the defendant would be great and the interference caused by the "invading" structure to the plaintiff is relatively slight), courts do often order the defendant to pay at least nominal damages.[5]

The major problem in modern times with the *ad coelum* dimension of the phrase has been the invention of air travel. Courts have created a variety of theories to give airplanes the right to fly over private property without being subject to countless trespass suits. On the whole, in the absence of an actionable nuisance, courts have limited a private property owner's interest to the airspace which s/he can reasonably use.[6] In *United States v. Causby*,[7] the U.S. Supreme Court held that "[f]lights over private land [by military planes] are not a taking [i.e., a taking of property without just compensation under the fifth amendment], unless they are so low and so frequent as to be a direct and immediate interference with the enjoyment and use of the land."[8] In *Causby*, U.S. Navy bombers, transports, and fighters regularly flew 67 feet over Causby's house, 63 feet over his barn, and 18 feet over his tallest tree. The noise and vibration terrified his chickens (Causby was a commercial chicken farmer). About 150 of his chickens, petrified by the planes, died when they flew into the walls of the barn. In short, his chicken business was ruined. The Supreme Court found that this invasion of Causby's *ad coelum* property interest did, in fact, constitute a fifth amendment taking violation.[9]

Courts have not yet eroded the *ad inferos* aspect of the *cujus est solum* doctrine to the same extent as the *ad coelum* part. The case *Edwards v. Lee's Administrator*[10] illustrates the application of the *ad inferos* principle.

Around 1916 Edwards discovered the entrance to a cave on his property. His cave was about three miles away from the well-known Kentucky tourist attraction, the Mammoth Cave. Edwards, looking to make a buck, began advertising his cave via signs and leaflets. In time his cave, which he dubbed the Great Onyx Cave (because of the onyx therein), turned into a reasonably profitable business for him. For example, in 1929 his net profit was $24,551.96 and in 1930, $23,340.51.[11] Years later, after the Mammoth Cave had been converted into a national park and the National Park Service had bought the Great Onyx Cave from Edwards, Lee, Edwards's neighbor (apparently a neighbor only in body not in spirit), claimed that, although the entrance to the Great Onyx Cave was on Edwards's property, part of it was underneath his (Lee's) land. Therefore, Lee sued Edwards for a portion of the profits which the cave had produced from 1923 to 1930. After a considerable amount of evidence had been presented, the court concluded that approximately one-third of the Great Onyx Cave, which had been open to the public, was actually under the surface of Lee's land.[12] Therefore, applying the doctrine *ad inferos*, the Kentucky Court of Appeals awarded Lee one-third of Edwards's profits plus 6% interest.[13]

My favorite comment about the phrase *cujus est solum* is in *Hannabalson v. Sessions*.[14] The judge in *Hannabalson* commented that, although "the title of the owner of the soil extends not only downward to the centre of the earth, but upward *usque ad coelum*," given the "quarrelsome" nature of the litigants in the case before him, it was doubtful that they would "ever enjoy the usufruct of their property in the latter direction."[15]

DONATIO CAUSA MORTIS & INTER VIVOS

The phrase, *donatio causa mortis* means "a gift by reason of death."[16] *Inter vivos* means "among the living."[17]

Law students meet these terms when they study gifts. Lawyers typically deal with these Latin phrases when working with estate planning and tax issues. When a person attempts to make a gift *inter vivos*, essentially three things must occur in order for the gift to be valid. First, the donor must intend to transfer the property (or interest in the property) in question; second, there must be a "delivery" of the property to the donee; and finally, the donee must intend to accept the gift. A valid *inter vivos* gift is irrevocable. Once the donor relinquishes his/her rights in the property, delivers the property to the donee, and the donee has accepted the gift, the property becomes the donee's.[18]

A succinct definition of gifts *causa mortis* is tricky. However, when an individual makes a gift of property to another person because s/he (the donor) is suffering from some condition (e.g., cancer, AIDS, a severe bullet wound, a cerebral hemorrhage, etc.) which s/he (i.e., the donor) believes will be fatal, such a gift is usually said to be *causa mortis* ("by reason of death").[19] The key factor which distinguishes gifts *inter vivos* from gifts *causa mortis* is that the latter are revocable. In order for a *donatio causa mortis* to be valid, the following events must occur: (1) the donor must be in such a condition that his/her death is imminent; (2) the donor must deliver the gift to the donee; (3) the donor must intend the gift to become effective only upon his/her death due to the condition which s/he is suffering; and (4) the donor must eventually die as a result of the condition which triggered his/her desire to give the gift.[20] Therefore, if the donor recovers from the condition from which s/he suffers, the gift is thereby revoked by operation of law.[21] If the donor should manifest an intent to revoke the gift before death, the gift is revoked.[22] If the donee should die before the donor dies, the gift is revoked.[23]

The discussion of both *inter vivos* and *causa mortis* gifts in *Titusville Trust Co. v. Johnson*[24] is particularly lucid. In *Titusville Trust* a junk dealer named Collins had a housekeeper, Johnson. Collins was stricken with a cerebral hemorrhage. After a doctor had been called, Collins handed Johnson an envelope and said: "If anything happens to me, these stocks are yours."[25] Johnson took the envelope from Collins. After being hospitalized, Collins died three days later. The court discussed both *inter vivos* and *causa mortis* gifts. "To establish a gift *inter vivos* . . . two essential elements must be made to appear: an intention to make the donation then and there, and an actual or constructive delivery at the same time, of a nature sufficient to divest the giver of all dominion, and invest the recipient therewith."[26] With respect to gifts *causa mortis* the court said,

> To validate a gift mortis causa, it is not necessary that the donor who is sick or ill or injured expressly say that he knows or believes he is dying—that may be inferred from the attendant circumstances. It will suffice if at the time the gift was made, the donor believed he was going to die, that he was likely to die soon; and death did actually ensue within a reasonable time thereafter.[27]

The Supreme Court of Pennsylvania thus held that Collins's gift of stocks to his housekeeper Johnson was a valid *donatio causa mortis*.[28]

Courts generally favor *inter vivos* gifts. They typically are biased against gifts *causa mortis* because such gifts tend to invade the territory otherwise occupied by wills.[29]

JUS TERTII

The phrase *jus tertii* means "the right of a third party."[30]

In order to understand this phrase in the context of property law, it is best to consider an example. Suppose that O (Owner), the owner of a gold ring, loses it. P (Possessor) finds it. O discovers that P has the ring and sues P to replevy (i.e., get back) the ring. P admits that s/he is not the original owner of the ring but claims that O is not really the true owner either. P claims that someone else (a third party) is the true owner. Thus, P claims that his/her claim to the ring (by virtue of having found it) is superior to the allegedly bogus claim of O. P's defense is called a *jus tertii* defense because s/he is claiming that the true ownership rests in some unnamed and unknown party.

As a general rule the *jus tertii* defense fails if the plaintiff can prove that s/he possessed the property in question before the defendant possessed it.[31] The defendant generally prevails on a theory of *jus tertii* only if s/he can prove that s/he (the defendant) possessed the property in question before the plaintiff.[32]

NEC VI, NEC CLAM, NEC PRECARIO

This Latin expression means "neither by force, nor secretly, nor given as a favor."[33] Old cases involving questions of adverse possession sometimes use this terminology to describe the means by which someone may acquire ownership of real property by openly possessing the land for a specified amount of time. Although jurisdictions vary somewhat, modern property law generally has adopted this Latin phrase but also has added to it. Most states today recognize that five elements must be present for an individual to succeed in acquiring title to property by adverse possession: (1) the individual must actually possess the property in question for a certain period of time (at common law this was usually twenty years but today either statutes or judicial decisions have shortened the period in many jurisdictions to fifteen years or less); (2) the individual must possess the property openly and notoriously "giving reasonable notice to the owner and the community" (*nec clam*); (3) the individual must possess the property continuously throughout the duration of the required time period; (4) the individual must possess the property without the owner's permission (*nec precario*); and (5) the individual must possess the property "under claim of right" (*nec vi*).[34] Thus, most jurisdictions require that an adverse possessor retain possession of the property continuously for a statutory period of time in addition to the open (*nec clam*), hostile (*nec precario*), and claim of right (*nec vi*) elements comprised in the common law Latin term.

There are numerous formulations of the doctrine of adverse possession, and different jurisdictions stress different elements. One early twentieth century case from New York articulated the "essential elements of adverse possession" as follows: "first, the possession must be hostile and under claim of right; second, it must be actual; third, it must be open and notorious; fourth, it must be exclusive; and fifth, it must be continuous."[35] I have even heard law students use the acronym O-C-E-A-N to memorize the elements of adverse possession: O-open; C-continuous; E-exclusive; A-actual; N-notorious.

The primary justification usually given for allowing a person to obtain title to property by adverse possession is to clear disputed titles. It is often said that the law does not protect those who "sleep on their rights." Thus, if a landowner abandons his/her property and either knowingly or unknowingly allows someone else to occupy it openly, continuously, exclusively claiming to own it, for a substantial period of time, it is reasonable that the law would extinguish the rights of the careless owner in favor of the person possessing and claiming the land.[36] In short, the law punishes the neglectful property owner and rewards the brazen, but persistent, trespasser. If an owner fails to eject the trespasser within the statute of limitations, s/he (the original owner) legally forfeits the land.

Law students typically examine cases that illustrate different interpretations of what constitutes open possession, claim of right, continuity of possession, length of possession, and the other elements in various jurisdictions. In practice, as in law school, the cases usually turn on the facts. Thus, it is critical to examine each element in an adverse possession claim carefully. The *nec vi, nec clam,* and *nec precario* components provide a good starting point in any adverse possession analysis. In addition to these three requirements in the Latin phrase, the time factors (both length and continuity) are now generally recognized as additional key elements for adverse possession.

RATIONE SOLI

The phrase *ratione soli* means "by reason of the soil."[37]

Ownership is a complex dimension of property law. People acquire ownership of property in a number of ways including by gift and by purchase. However, people acquire some things by merely possessing them (i.e., by having the property in their control and intending to keep it). We can acquire ownership of wild animals (*ferae naturae*), personal property (typically property which another person has lost), and real property by means of possession.[38]

Landowners are said to own the fruits of the land and the wild animals on it by title *ratione soli*. In other words, because they own the land, they, therefore, own all of the things on the land as well.

For example, in the famous case *Pierson v. Post*[39] (where Post was fox hunting—with hounds, etc.—and was in hot pursuit of one particular fox, when Pierson interceded, caught the fox, and killed it), Judge Tompkins noted that in English precedents when hunters had caught wild animals on another's property, the landowners ordinarily claimed title to the animals under the principle of *ratione soli*.[40]

The seminal case in English jurisprudence that states the concept of *ratione soli*, *Blades v. Higgs*,[41] holds: "Property *ratione soli* is the common law right which every owner of land has to kill and take all such animals ferae naturae as may from time to time be found on his land, and as soon as this right is exercised the animal so killed or caught becomes the absolute property of the owner of the soil."[42]

The Restatement of Property provides as follows:

> By virtue of his possession, a possessor of land occupies a favored position with respect to some things which are for the time being within the space comprehended by his possession, but which may be regarded as not yet having been reduced to possession. Included among such things are those wild birds and wild animals which have not been appropriated and which are in general open to appropriation. If such things come within the space possessed by a possessor of land, his right of exclusive occupation of the land enables him to prevent, for the time being, an appropriation by others. Subject to such paramount au-

thority as may be asserted by the state, he not only has this power to prevent appropriation by others, but an attempt at appropriation by others may be rendered ineffective by his right to claim the benefit of the attempt. Thus, if B, a trespasser, shoots wild game upon land possessed by A, A may claim the game or recover damages for its conversion.[43]

Title *ratione soli* may be viewed, in one sense, as a kind of natural right to ownership by the owner of real property.

SIC UTERE TUO UT ALIENUM NON LAEDAS

This Latin maxim means "use your own [property] in such a way that you do not harm another."[44]

This phrase is a capsulized version of the underpinning of the law of private nuisance. Before a court determines that one landowner is using his/her property in such a way that s/he is injuring others, it generally considers a number of factors. According to Prosser, "[t]he essence of private nuisance is an interference with the use and enjoyment of land."[45] It is possible to use one's property in such a way that it harms others in a variety of ways (e.g., blasting, flooding, polluting, burning rubbish, emitting gases, causing loud noises, etc.). "So long as the interference is substantial and unreasonable, and such as would be offensive or inconvenient to the normal person, virtually any disturbance of the enjoyment of the property may amount to a nuisance."[46]

The most common remedies available for private nuisance are an injunction or a payment of money damages.[47] Courts have traditionally "balanced the equities" involved in order to decide whether an injunction or a payment of money damages is appropriate.[48] Generally speaking, before a court will enjoin a nuisance, a plaintiff must first show that the defendant's disturbance is unreasonable given the surrounding circumstances.[49]

A case which is probably in every current first-year property casebook is *Boomer v. Atlantic Cement Co., Inc.*[50] In *Boomer* the plaintiffs were landowners living near a cement plant. They sued because of the plant's dust and blasting. The cement plant employed over 300 local residents and played a vital role in the town's economy. The court granted a temporary injunction but ordered that the injunction be suspended if Atlantic Cement agreed to pay some $185,000 in permanent damages to the landowners/plaintiffs.[51] In a vigorous dissent, Judge Jasen lamented, "I see grave dangers in overruling our long-established rule of granting an injunction where nuisance results in substantial continuing damage. In permitting the injunction to become inoperative upon the payment of permanent damages, the majority is, in effect, licensing a continuing wrong."[52]

It should be noted that a great many national environmental statutes (e.g., The Clean Air Act, the Clean Water Act, etc.) are becoming the principal anti-pollution weapons in our society rather than nuisance actions.

Nevertheless, the maxim *sic utere tuo ut alienum non laedas* is applicable to the modern environmental statutes just as it is applicable to the common law theory of private nuisance.

■ ENDNOTES

1. The key words in this Latin phrase are *solum* ("land, earth, soil"), *usque* ("all the way"), *ad* ("to"), *coelum* (a medieval version of the classical word *caelum*, "sky, heaven"), and *inferos* ("the lowest regions, the underworld"). For this and several other rather lengthy Latin maxims, I depart from my usual custom of translating and explaining each word in the Latin term. For such long phrases, I suspect that a tedious explanation of the translation would probably bore rather than enlighten.

2. Coke called his treatise the *Institutes* after Roman treatises by Gaius and Justinian of the same name.

3. *See,* e.g., *Geragosian v. Union Realty Co.*, 289 Mass. 104, 193 N.E. 726, (1935).

4. W. Prosser & W. Keeton, The Law of Torts, § 13 at 81 (5th ed. 1984) [hereinafter Prosser and Keeton].

5. *See* McCormick, Damages 90 (1935) (Citing cases where courts awarded nominal damages, e.g., *Bungerstock v. Nishnabotna Drainage Dist.*, 163 Mo. 198, 64 S.W. 149 (1901) and *Swift v.Broyles*, 115 Ga. 885, 42 S.E. 277 (1902)).

6. The Restatement (Second) of Torts § 194 generally upholds the *cujus est solum* doctrine but makes an exception for aircraft. According to the Restatement, an airplane is exempted from the *cujus est solum* doctrine unless the flight occurs within the immediate reaches of the land and the aircraft substantially interferes with the owner's use and enjoyment of the land.

7. 328 U.S. 256 (1946).

8. *Id.* at 266.

9. *Id.* at 267.

10. 265 Ky. 418, 96 S.W.2d 1028 (1936). *Also see Sui Generis* in Chapter Nine, *infra.*

11. 265 Ky. 418, 421, 96 S.W.2d at 1029.

12. *Id.*

13. *Id.* at 429, 96 S.W.2d at 1033.

14. 116 Iowa 457, 90 N.W. 93 (1902).

15. *Id.* at 461, 90 N.W. at 95.

16. The noun *donatio* simply means "a gift." *Causa* is here in the ablative case and thus means "by reason." *Mortis* is the genitive singular of the Latin noun *mors* ("death") and, as such, means "of death."

17. *Inter* is a preposition meaning "between" or "among." *Vivos* is used here as a substantive of the verb *vivere* ("to live") in the accusative plural (the preposition *inter* requires the accusative case) meaning "the living" or "those people who are living."

18. Law students ordinarily study the intricacies of determining the donor's intent and the subtleties of "delivery." Delivery is a particularly fascinating aspect of property law. Must a donor physically hand a car over to the donee, or will delivery of the keys be sufficient? Common sense tells us that the keys are enough, and that, of course, is generally true. Nevertheless, the problems and pitfalls of delivering property can be complex.

19. *See generally J.* Cribbet and C. Johnson, Principles of the Law of Property 155 (3d ed. 1989).

20. *See generally R.* Brown, The Law Of Personal Property § 7.15-§ 7.20 at 130-45 (3d ed. 1975). *Also see Newman v. Bost,* 122 N.C. 324, 20 S.E. 848 (1898).

21. Boyer, Survey of the Law of Property 699 (3d ed. 1981). *Also see Allen v. Hendrick,* 104 Or. 202, 219, 206 P. 733, 738 (1922).

22. *Allen v. Hendrick,* 104 Or. 202, 219 (1922).

23. *Id.*

24. 375 Pa. 493, 100 A.2d 93 (1953).

25. 100 A. 2d 93 at 97.

26. 100 A.2d 93, 96-97. Of course the donee would have to accept the gift in order to "invest therewith."

27. *Id.* at 97.

28. *Id.* at 98.

29. R. Brown, *supra* note 20, § 7.20, at 144.

30. In Latin the noun *jus* means "law" or "right." *Tertii* is the genitive singular of the ordinal numeral *tertius* ("third"). In this phrase *tertii* is used as a substantive to mean "a third person" or a "third party."

31. C. Donahue, Jr., T. Kauper, and P. Martin, Cases and Materials on Property 57 (2d ed. 1983).

32. There are exceptions to the general rule; the *jus tertii* defense sometimes succeeds in certain circumstances. Nevertheless, the general inadequacy of the *jus tertii* defense illustrates the legal importance of possession. A person who finds property and keeps it in his/her possession has a claim to that property superior to all others except the true owner.

33. The successive occurrences of *nec* mean "neither . . . nor . . . nor." *Vi* is the ablative singular of the noun *vis* ("force, strength"). Here *vi* is an ablative of means and is best translated in English as "by force" or "by means of force." *Clam* is an adverb meaning "secretly" or "under cover." *Precario*, like *vi*, is an ablative of means; the ablative singular substantive form of the adjective, *precarius,-a,-um*.

34. C. Harr and L. Liebman, Property and Law 80 (2d ed. 1985).

35. *Belotti v. Bickhardt*, 228 N.Y. 296, 127 N.E. 239 (1920).

36. It is interesting to note that the doctrine of adverse possession conflicts with another Latin maxim, *primus in tempore potior est in jure* ("first in time is more powerful in law"). When the *primus in tempore* abandons the property and allows an adverse possessor to occupy the property for the statutory period, s/he, in effect, loses his/her "more powerful" status ordinarily conferred by law.

37. The Latin noun *ratio* means "reason." *Ratione* is the ablative singular of *ratio* and thus here means "by reason." *Soli* is the genitive singular of *solum* ("soil, ground, earth, land") and means "of the soil."

38. R. Brown, *supra* note 20, § 15, at 6.

39. 3 Cai. R. 175, 2 Am. Dec. 264 (N.Y. 1805).

40. *Id.* at 265.

41. 11 H.L.C. 619, 11 English Reprint 1474 (1865).

42. *Id.* at 630, 11 English Reprint at 1478.

43. Restatement of Property § 450 comment, "Use or Enjoyment—Exclusive privilege of appropriation" at 2906 (1944).

44. *Utere* is the singular imperative of the deponent verb *utor* ("to use"). *Tuo* is the ablative singular of the second-person singular adjective *tuus* ("yours") and here is used as a substantive meaning "your own [property]." *Tuo* is ablative because the verb *utor* ordinarily takes the ablative case as its object. *Sic* means "thus" or "in such a way" and helps to introduce the result clause that follows. *Ut* simply means "that." *Laedas* is the present subjunctive second-person singular of the verb *laedere* ("to injure" or "to harm") and thus means "you harm." *Alienum* is the accusative singular of the adjective, *alienus* ("another's") and here is the direct object of *laedas*. *Non* means "not."

45. Prosser and Keeton *supra* note 4, at 619.

46. *Id.* at 620.

47. *Id.* at 641.

48. *See* Cunningham, Stoebuck, and Whitman, The Law of Property at § 7.2, at 417 (1984).

49. Prosser and Keeton *supra* note 4, at 641.
50. 257 N.E.2d 870 (N.Y. 1970).
51. *Id.* at 875.
52. *Id.* at 876.

CHAPTER EIGHT

TORTS

■ THE ROMAN BACKGROUND

In ancient Rome there never was a specific body of law precisely analogous to modern tort law. Interestingly enough, the etymology of the word "tort" has its origins in the Latin verb *torquere* (the fourth principal part of *torquere* is *tortum*) meaning "to twist, wind, wrench." It also can mean "to hurl violently, whirl" and even "to rack, torture, torment." *Tortum*, then, means "that which has been twisted, wound, wrenched." Prosser explains the derivation by saying that "a tort is conduct which is twisted, or crooked, not straight."[1] Scholars agree that there is no universally satisfactory definition of a tort. Nevertheless, by knowing the Latin underpinnings of the word, it is easier to grasp the overall concept.

In ancient Roman jurisprudence, the closest thing to modern tort law was a body of law which came under the classification of *obligationes ex delicto* ("obligations arising out of a crime, fault, or delinquency"). However, unlike modern tort law, in which damages are generally intended to put the injured party back into the same position in which s/he would have been if the tort had never occurred, damages resulting from *obligationes ex delicto* were almost always penal, usually exacting multiple damages.

There were at least eight major types of *obligationes ex delicto* recognized in ancient Rome. In classical civil law there were four: (1) *injuria* (notably: assault, battery, and defamation); (2) *furtum* ("theft"); (3) *rapina* (essentially aggravated theft); and (4) *damnum injuria datum* (property damage—especially damage to slaves and livestock). The praetors (the pre-eminent judicial officials in ancient Rome) created a number of other *obligationes ex delicto* in addition to those traditionally recognized in the *jus civile* (civil law). Similarly, courts and judges today continue to create new torts. For example, intentional infliction of emotional harm, invasion of privacy, and infringement of a person's right of publicity are all relatively new theories of tort. The Roman praetors created four types of *delicts* particularly worthy of note: (1) *metus* (threats of physical harm); (2) *dolus* (fraud); (3) *servi corruptio* ("corruption of a slave," e.g., teaching a slave how to rob or cheat); and (4) *alienatio in fraudem creditorum* (selling one's property in order to defraud creditors).

The Romans also recognized certain *obligationes quasi ex delicto* ("obligations as if arising out of fault, crime, delinquency"). Three such *obligationes* are quite similar to modern torts which impose strict liability or torts which the present law observes as *res ipsa loquitur*: (1) *actio de rebus effusis vel dejectis* (literally "an action concerning things being poured or thrown down") (if something was poured or thrown out of an owner's premises onto a common way and injured another person or the property of another, the owner was held strictly liable); (2) *actio de posito et suspenso* (literally "an action concerning that which has been placed and that which has been hung") (if an owner placed or suspended something, like a sign, which endangered travelers on the road, the owner was held strictly liable); (3) another obligation imposed strict liability on those in charge of ships, inns, and stables for injuries which were incurred by persons or animals under their control.

Thus, a great many of our modern notions of tort originated in the ancient Roman legal concepts of *obligationes delicto* and *quasi ex delicto*.

Modern tort law encompasses many different legal theories. As was mentioned above, there is no one all-inclusive definition of what a tort is. We generally identify torts as civil wrongs. In law school, students customarily study individual "types" of torts such as assault, battery, negligence, strict liability, products liability, and defamation.

CONSORTIUM

Consortium is a Latin noun which means a "partnership." Its origin is actually in the word *sors* ("share" or "lot").[2]

Lawyers and law students meet the word *consortium* primarily in the phrase "loss of *consortium*." The meaning of *consortium*, or partnership in this context, refers to the loss of affection, support, services, and general companionship suffered by members of a family when the conduct of some third party injures or kills another member of the same immediate family.

In the English common law, the first loss of *consortium* which courts recognized was for a husband whose wife had been injured in such a way that she was unable to have sex with him or take care of the household.[3] Since the wife could no longer perform certain "services" for the husband, he was entitled to the value of those "services" from the tortfeasor. A wife, on the other hand, whose husband was injured, could not recover in a similar fashion. This less-than-enlightened (i.e., sexist) attitude developed because the husband-wife relationship was considered to be essentially a master-servant relationship.

It was not until the 1950s that most United States courts began recognizing a wife's cause of action for loss of *consortium* against a tortfeasor whose conduct had injured her husband. According to Prosser, today "[a]ny tort causing direct physical injury to one spouse will give rise to a claim for loss of consortium by the other."[4]

It is important to distinguish a claim for loss of *consortium* from a claim for medical expenses incurred. *Consortium* compensates a loss of companionship and "services." Medical fees, although generally recoverable under a separate theory, are not included within the scope of loss of *consortium*.

Now that courts generally recognize that a wife has a claim for loss of *consortium* on par with a husband, the real battleground in the field of loss of *consortium* has shifted. Today the cutting-edge issue is whether parents may recover for loss of *consortium* due to injuries suffered by their children and vice versa.

As regards the claim of a parent which is based upon an injury to his/her child, the Restatement (Second) of Torts, § 703, Comment (h) provides that a parent cannot recover for loss of *consortium* in cases where the child was injured negligently. Nevertheless, in cases where the child has died, and the parents bring their claim in a wrongful death action, many courts have allowed bereaved parents to recover against the tortfeasor for loss of *consortium*. However, where the action is based upon an injury alone, a plaintiff/parent is highly unlikely to persuade a court to even listen to the case.

Until recently children who sought damages for loss of *consortium* due to injuries to their parents usually were unable to recover. However, in the early 1980s several states began recognizing a child's loss of *consortium* claim based upon parental injury.[5]

DAMNUM ABSQUE INJURIA

The phrase *damnum absque injuria* means "loss without injustice," or "injury without wrong."[6]

Our society today is decidedly litigious. People want to sue others over what seem to be the slightest matters. We tend to forget (especially as law students and lawyers) that some accidents are unavoidable. Sometimes, even though everyone is acting reasonably, people just get hurt. Under these circumstances, the injured party (or his/her insurer) must bear the costs without compensation from a third party.

The phrase *damnum absque injuria* describes those situations when, although someone suffers damage, that damage does not give rise to a legal cause of action. Thus, the word "injury," as it is used in the law of torts, really means damage which is caused by some wrongful or unlawful act. If a person picks up a stick to defend him/herself from an attacking dog and happens to strike a bystander, the damage to the bystander would, more likely than not, be considered *damnum absque injuria*.[7] The person being attacked was acting in a reasonable and lawful manner. In fact, whenever a person is doing anything which is lawful or is exercising a legal right, and someone else is inadvertently injured as a result, that injury is ordinarily not the type of injury which is actionable.

PER SE

Per se means "by itself."[8]

Although the phrase *per se* may appear in many different legal contexts, one of the most common places to find it is in tort law. "Negligence *per se*" and "slander *per se*" for example, are two theories of tort upon which plaintiffs commonly rely in litigation. Generally speaking, when an action is characterized as *per se*, the court waives the necessity for the plaintiff to produce certain types of evidence. The court simply demands less proof from the plaintiff.

"Negligence *per se*" is a good example. Most jurisdictions agree that if a defendant has violated a statute and if the plaintiff, who was injured as a result of the defendant's violation of that statute, was a member of the class of persons whom that statute was designed to protect, then the defendant's violation of that statute is considered negligence *per se*.[9] Thus, in order to prevail, the plaintiff need prove nothing more than that the defendant's conduct violated the statute, that the defendant's conduct caused the plaintiff's injury, and that s/he (the plaintiff) is the type of person whom the statute was intended to protect. In such cases, the plaintiff is not required to prove the ordinary elements which comprise a *prima facie* case for negligence (duty, breach, proximate/legal cause, and injury in fact) in order to recover. Instead, the defendant's conduct is conclusively deemed negligent by itself (*per se*). The existence of a statute replaces the duty component in ordinary negligence.

Osborne v. McMasters[8] is a classic case of negligence *per se*, which appears in many tort casebooks. In *Osborne* the defendant, a druggist, sold a bottle containing poison to the plaintiff by mistake. A Minnesota statute mandated that all bottles sold containing poison had to be labeled with appropriate warnings. The plaintiff died after drinking the poison. The court held that the defendant's violation of the compulsory labeling statute constituted negligence *per se*.[11] In other words, because the defendant failed to label the bottle of poison properly as required by the statute, his failure to act was negligence by itself and, thus, the plaintiff did not have to prove the standard elements of negligence.

Another good example of how the term *per se* is used in tort law is "slander *per se*." For a number of reasons, many of which are historical, two types of slander have developed in the law of defamation: ordinary slander and slander *per se*.[12] In an action for ordinary slander, a plaintiff is generally required to plead and prove special damage in order to prevail. Special damage is difficult to prove because a plaintiff must show pecuniary loss with a certain degree of exactitude. However, four exceptions to the requirement of proving special damage evolved. These four exceptions have come to be called slanders *per se*.[13]

This "carving out" of slanders *per se* has traditionally been crucial to a plaintiff's case. Unless a plaintiff can prove that the slander complained of is *per se*, all other things that a person might say, no matter how defamatory or insulting they might be, are only actionable if the plaintiff can prove special damages (i.e., the plaintiff must offer proof of specific pecuniary loss resulting from the defendant's defamatory statement). On the other hand, if the slander complained of is actionable *per se*, plaintiffs have been able, traditionally, to recover general damages (e.g., for injury to reputation, loss of business, wounded feelings, and bodily suffering), which are merely presumed to exist without actual proof of those damages. Although not all courts have agreed on this issue, the majority of courts have held that punitive damages (i.e., damages awarded due to the malicious nature of the defendant's conduct) are always available in actions for slander *per se*.[14] However, for all other slanders (i.e., ordinary, non-*per se* slander), punitive damages are only available upon proof of special damages.[15]

RES IPSA LOQUITUR

The phrase *res ipsa loquitur* literally means "the thing, itself, speaks."[16]

The phrase *res ipsa loquitur* relates to a broader concept of tort, namely, negligence. As was noted above, in order to prove negligence, a plaintiff ordinarily must prove duty, breach, injury, and proximate/legal causation.[17] We have also seen that in cases involving negligence *per se*, the plaintiff's burden of proof is significantly less than it is under normal circumstances.[18] The doctrine of *res ipsa loquitur* is, in many respects, similar to negligence *per se*. In cases where the doctrine of *res ipsa loquitur* applies, the plaintiff's burden of proof changes—s/he does not have to prove the ordinary elements of *prima facie* case of negligence.

What is involved is circumstantial evidence. There are occasions when a plaintiff simply cannot prove, by direct testimony, that a defendant was negligent. When there are no eyewitnesses available, a plaintiff must use circumstantial evidence as well as s/he can. If certain other circumstances exist, most American jurisdictions will allow a plaintiff to prove his/her case with only circumstantial evidence under a theory of *res ipsa loquitur*. It is when those other certain circumstances exist that the doctrine of *res ipsa loquitur* applies.

First, it must be clear that the type of injury sustained by the plaintiff ordinarily does not happen unless someone is negligent. Prosser lists injuries such as those sustained when bricks or window panes fall from the defendant's premises, when elevators fall, when animals escape onto the highway, when gases escape from pipes, when wheels suddenly detach from moving vehicles, when buses, trains, or planes crash, when foods sealed in containers poison people, and many others.[19] Number two, whatever it was that caused the injury must have been, or should have been, in the exclusive control of the defendant. For example, a plane which crashes should be in the control of the airline; a farmer should be in control of his cattle which cause an auto accident after straying onto a road; a cereal manufacturer should be in control of what goes into its cereal boxes. And finally, the plaintiff must show that s/he was not the negligent party.[20]

The case which appears in most law school casebooks to introduce *res ipsa loquitur* is the seminal *res ipsa* case, *Byrne v. Boadle.*[21] Here, our poor friend Byrne was walking down the street one day minding his own business, when a barrel full of flour fell on his head out of Boadle's shop window from above. Do you know how much a barrel (not just a sack, mind you, but a barrel) full of flour weighs? Neither do I but the case only tells us that he "was helpless for a fortnight."[22] So there you have it. Let us now compare the elements which are necessary for a case of *res ipsa loquitur* against the facts in *Byrne v. Boadle.* (1) First, barrels of flour ordinarily do not fall from windows and smash passersby on the street unless someone was negligent. Therefore, this injury occurred in such a way that negligence is ordinarily involved. (2) Barrels full of flour in a shop are generally under or should be under the complete control of the shopowner (or his/her agents). Thus, the thing which caused the injury was in the exclusive control of the defendant, Boadle. (3) It is clear that Byrne was not at fault. To be sure, if he had not been walking down the street at that particular time the flour barrel would not have clobbered him. Nevertheless, merely walking down the street does not make him negligent. Plaintiffs will always be doing *something* when they are injured, but that conduct does not necessarily make them contributorily negligent. Therefore, as Chief Baron Pollock, who authored the decision in *Byrne v. Boadle* stated, "There are certain cases of which it may be said *res ipsa loquitur* and this seems one of them."[23]

ONDEAT SUPERIOR

rase *respondeat superior* literally means "Let the one above [4]

The tort doctrine of *respondeat superior* is also sometimes called "vicarious liability."[25] Let us start with an example. Suppose that you are out for an afternoon drive. You are taking your time and driving carefully. Suddenly a delivery girl, driving a car with a sign on top reading "Sally & Bobby's Pizza—Fast Delivery," runs a red light and collides with your car. To make matters interesting, let us assume that you are severely injured in the crash (a concussion, a few broken ribs, a broken ankle, a dislocated shoulder). Furthermore, in addition to the damage done directly to you and your car (broken glass, dents, etc.), your backseat is plastered in tomato sauce, mozzarella cheese, sausage, and other assorted toppings. In a situation such as this, where the pizza-delivery girl is only 17 years old and makes minimum wage, you may be unable to recover all of your expenses just from her. Here, the law steps in and applies the doctrine of *respondeat superior*: Let the one (or in this case, the ones, i.e., Sally and Bobby) reply. The notion is actually fairly simple. If the "servant" is acting within the scope of his/her employment, the "master" becomes vicariously liable for the servant's negligence. In other words, the servant's negligence is imputed to the master. In our example of Sally & Bobby's Pizza, it is clear from the facts that the delivery girl was acting within the scope of her employment when she ran the red light and smashed into you. The pizza debris that landed in the back of your car is pretty good evidence that she was acting within the scope of her employment (i.e., attempting to deliver pizzas—after all the sign did say "Fast Delivery," didn't it?) when the accident occurred.[26]

Although courts have advanced several noble-sounding explanations to support the doctrine of *respondeat superior* (e.g., the master is, in one sense, in control of his/her servants;[27] the master screened his/her servants before hiring them and, thus, should accept the responsibility for their negligent acts),[28] nevertheless, the "deep pocket" explanation is probably as realistic as any.[29] Sally and Bobby are in a better position to pay for your losses than the delivery girl.[30]

In order for the doctrine of *respondeat superior* to apply, the plaintiff must first establish that the employee's negligence proximately caused his/her injuries, and then must prove that the employee was acting within the scope of his/her employment. If the employee was not acting within the scope of his/her employment, the superior (i.e., the employer) cannot be vicariously liable.[31] For example, in the pizza hypothetical above, if the delivery girl had simply been using the company car on her own time (e.g., to run errand and not to deliver pizzas), Sally & Bobby would not have been liable under the theory of *respondeat superior*. Determining whether the employee was acting within the scope of his/her employment is generally the pivotal problem in cases where a plaintiff claims that *respondeat superior* should apply.[32]

VOLENTI NON FIT INJURIA

The phrase *volenti non fit injuria* means "a wrong does not come into existence for one who is willing."[33]

This Latin phrase expresses the tort concept which is also called "assumption of risk."[34] Assumption of risk is a defense to alleged negligence. If a defendant can prove that the injured plaintiff understood that s/he (i.e., the plaintiff) was involved in a potentially dangerous situation to begin with, and that s/he, aware of and appreciating the nature of the risk involved, still proceeded to take part in the potentially dangerous activity, then the defendant ought not be held liable.[35] In simple terms, if a person has voluntarily undertaken a task fully understanding that the task may result in injury, s/he cannot later claim that compensation is owed for an injury caused by the negligence of another while involved in that task. The plaintiff in such a case is said to have assumed the risk.

The case *Hildebrand v. Minyard*[36] summarizes the generally accepted elements necessary in order for the doctrine of assumption of risk to apply: "(1) There must be a risk of harm to the plaintiff caused by the defendant's conduct or by the condition of the defendant's land or chattels; (2) Plaintiff must have actual knowledge of the particular risk and appreciate its magnitude; (3) The plaintiff must voluntarily choose to enter or remain within the area of the risk under circumstances that manifest his willingness to accept that particular risk."[37]

A person can expressly assume a risk (for example, by signing a waiver in a contract) or impliedly assume a risk (as evidenced by conduct). In either case, the assumption of the risk must be voluntary and with knowledge of the potential hazards involved. Prosser observes that "those who participate or sit as spectators at sports and amusements may be taken to assume the known risks of being hurt by roller coasters, flying baseballs, hockey pucks, golf balls, wrestlers, or such things as fireworks explosions."[38]

The cutting-edge topic today in the area of assumption of risk is the *effect* of proving that a plaintiff assumed a risk. In modern tort law an increasing number of jurisdictions are accepting the notion of pure comparative negligence.[39] In other words, to the extent that the trier of fact determines that the plaintiff him/herself is negligent, the defendant is not liable for that percentage of the injury. The earlier, traditional view at common law held that, if the plaintiff had been contributorily negligent, the defendant had a complete defense and was totally off the hook.[40] Under the theory of pure comparative negligence, each party is responsible for the *pro rata* proportion of the damage caused by his/her conduct. Therefore, if a jury were to determine that an injured plaintiff's injuries were worth $100,000, and that the plaintiff was 55% negligent and the defendant 45% negligent, the defendant would owe the plaintiff $45,000 in damages. Other jurisdictions use 50% as a dividing line and will not allow a plaintiff to recover anything if s/he is more than 50% negligent.[41]

It seems clear that assumption of risk will not absolve a defendant of all liability in a jurisdiction which observes pure comparative negligence. A comparative negligence jurisdiction is likely to apportion damages based upon the relative percentages of the negligence of either party. Thus, assumption of risk, in most jurisdictions, is probably no longer a complete bar to recovery by a plaintiff.

■ ENDNOTES

1. W. Prosser & W. Keeton, The Law of Torts, 931 (5th ed. 1984) [hereinafter Prosser & Keeton].
2. We also get the English word "sortition," "selection by lot" from *sors*. With the prefix *con*, forming the word *consors*, it means "having an equal share or lot."
3. Prosser and Keeton *supra* note 1, at 931.
4. *Id.* at 932.

5. *See, e.g., Ferriter v. Daniel O'Connell's Sons, Inc.*, 381 Mass. 507, 413 N.E. 2d 690 (1980); 11 *Berger v. Weber*, 411 Mich. 1, 303 N.W.2d 424 (1981); *Reighley v. International Playtex, Inc.*, 604 F. Supp. 1078 (D. Colo., 1985); *Kelly v. T.L. James Co.*, 603 F. Supp. 390 (W.D. La. 1985); *Weitl v. Moes*, 311 N.W.2d 259 (1981). It appears that the trend is to allow such actions on a more liberal basis than before.

6. This Latin phrase offers a simple lesson: merely because a person is damaged in some way does not necessarily mean that s/he has a legal cause of action against another. This concept offers a bit of common sense. In law school and in the legal profession in general we often get so wrapped up in the process that we forget that people can be hurt even though everyone is acting reasonably and lawfully.

7. *See Brown v. Kendall*, 60 Mass. (6 Cush.) 292 (1850).

8. *Per* is a Latin preposition meaning "through" or "by means of." In this particular phrase, the word *se* is the accusative singular form of the Latin reflexive pronoun (*sui, sibi, se, se*) and means "itself." *See* Chapter Six, *supra*, for a discussion of the Latin phrase *prima facie*.

9. *See* Restatement (Second) of Torts §§ 285-88c; and § 874A (1987), "Tort Liability for Violation of Legislative Provision."

10. 41 N.W. 543 (Minn. 1889).

11. *Id.* at 544.

12. *See generally* Morris, Morris on Torts 361-62 (2d ed. 1980).

13. These four types of slanders *per se* (which do not require a plaintiff to prove special harm in order to recover) arise when a defendant has made: (1) false statements imputing criminal behavior to the plaintiff; (2) false allegations that the plaintiff is currently suffering from a venereal or other loathsome or communicable disease; (3) false allegations adversely reflecting on the plaintiff's fitness to conduct his/her business, profession, trade, or office; and (4) false allegations accusing the plaintiff of sexual misconduct.

14. C. McCormick, Damages 415-16 (2d ed. 1935).

15. *Id.*

16. In this Latin phrase, the noun *res* ("thing") is in the nominative case and is the subject of the verb *loquitur* (the third-person singular of the deponent verb *loqui* which means "to speak"). *Ipsa* is an intensifying pronoun in the nominative case and here means "itself."

Everyone whom I know in the legal profession translates this phrase "the thing speaks for itself." This translation, although preserving the flavor of the original Latin, is technically incorrect. As was noted above, the pronoun *ipsa* is in the nominative case and therefore is an appositive. That is, *ipsa* is in apposition with *res*.

I have a fantasy that goes like this. It is midway through the fall semester of the first year in law school. The torts professor stands before the class and introduces the topic of *Res Ipsa Loquitur*. "Now, since I'm sure that none of you is educated well enough to have ever studied Latin, I'll tell you what this means. *Res ipsa loquitur* means "the thing speaks for itself." Suddenly a student stands near the back of the room (we'll call this brave student Nina) and addresses the professor.

> But professor, that simply can't be right. You see *ipsa* is an intensifying pronoun in the nominative case and therefore is in apposition with *res*. The Latin actually means "the thing, itself, speaks." In fact, professor, your translation is absolutely slipshod. You said "the thing speaks *for* itself." Now if it really said "*for* itself," the intensifying pronoun would perhaps be in the dative case, the case of the indirect object. That would be "*res sibi loquitur*" now, wouldn't it? Or perhaps it would be more accurate to use *pro* plus the ablative, "*res pro se loquitur*." Yes. That might be closer to your translation. In short, professor, I'm simply astonished that you could stand before us today and be so patently wrong. Do you always lie to all of your classes like this? I wonder what other lies have you told us?

Three comments about this fantasy. Number one, if you are a first-year law student, I really do hope that you will have the guts to be the Nina in your torts class. You may not want to be as heavy-handed as she is in my fantasy, but even lofty law professors need to be taken down a notch or two occasionally. Second, Nina deserves a standing ovation. Your torts professor has probably been intimidating the entire class for most of the semester up until now. It is time for the students to do a little intimidating of their own. And thirdly, if you do decide to be Nina in your torts class, be damned sure to read the next few paragraphs of this section which explain the tort doctrine, *res ipsa loquitur*. You can bet that any professor who takes a whipping, like the one that this little Latin lesson will give, will immediately reply, "OK, Mr./Ms. Latin scholar-know-it-all, since you know so much about *res ipsa loquitur*, perhaps you can explain to the class the next dozen cases you were to have prepared for today."

17. *See* Chapter Six, Evidence, *Prima Facie, supra.*

18. *See Per Se, supra.*

17. Prosser and Keeton *supra* note 1 at 244-45.

20. For example, a plaintiff who is cut while trying to open a soft drink bottle with a wrench instead of a bottle opener will not be able to prove that s/he is pure-as-the-driven-snow and thus will probably not be allowed to prove his/her case under the theory of *res ipsa loquitur*. (This really happened! *See Douglas v. Coca-Cola Bottling Co.*, 356 So. 2d 1054 (1978)).

21. 2 H. & C. 722, 159 Eng. Rep. 299 (1863).

22. *Id.*

23. *Id.* at 725. There will, of course, be variations on the theme, but the elements are the same. Lawyers must be sensitive to the possibility

that a fact pattern may fit the doctrine of *res ipsa loquitur*. If so, the plaintiff need not prove the ordinary elements of a *prima facie* case for negligence. Circumstantial evidence, in cases of *res ipsa loquitur*, is all that is necessary to shift the burden of proof to the defendant.

One professor responding to my original survey said that a student had once complained, "If the thing speaks for itself, why doesn't it speak in English?" Others have asked, *"Res ipsa loquitur, sed quid in inferos dicet?"* ("The thing itself speaks, but what in hell does it say?"). By now I hope you realize (1) that the thing doesn't speak *for* itself; rather, the thing itself speaks; (2) that it doesn't have to speak in English in order for intelligent people to understand it; and (3) what in hell it says!

24. *Respondeat* is the third-person singular present tense, active subjunctive (here a hortatory subjunctive) of the verb *respondere* ("to reply," "to give an official answer or opinion"). As such, *respondeat* means "let him/her/it reply." *Superior* is the comparative form of the adjective *superus* ("situated above") and thus means "upper" or "higher." Furthermore, in this phrase the adjective *superior* is a substantive and therefore means "one who is in a higher position."

25. *See, e.g.*, *Fruit v. Schreiner*, 502 P.2d 133 (1973).

26. *Cf. Lundberg v. State*, 306 N.Y.S.2d 947, 255 N.E.2d, 177, (1969) (holding that an employee of the state of New York was not acting within the scope of his employment when driving from his home to work on an engineering project—even though the state reimbursed the employee for travel and living expenses incurred while away from home).

27. *Fruit v. Schreiner*, 502 P.2d 133 at 139.

28. *Id.*

29. *Id.*

30. To be sure, Sally & Bobby probably have more dough than the delivery girl. Economists generally like the doctrine of *respondeat superior*. According to them, this doctrine yields an efficient allocation of resources. The employer is said to be the "superior risk bearer" because s/he/it is generally in a better position to insure against risk of loss than either the employee or the innocent victim. *See* Sykes, *The Economics of Vicarious Liability*, 93 Yale L.J. 1231 (1984). *See also* R. Posner, Economic Analysis of Law § 6.8 at 171 (3d ed. 1986).

31. *See* Restatement (Second) of Agency § 219 (2). *See* also e.g., *Lundberg v. State*, 306 N.Y.S.2d 947, 950; 255 N.E. 2d 177, 178.

32. *Fruit v. Schreiner*, 502 P.2d 133 at 140.

33. *Injuria* in this phrase is probably best translated "wrong." Here, I mean wrong in the sense of a legally redressable wrong. The verb *fit* (whose subject is *injuria*) is the third-person singular present of *fieri* ("to be made," "to come into existence") meaning "s/he, it comes into existence." *Non* simply means "not." *Volenti* is the present active participle of the verb *velle*

("to be willing," "to wish") in the dative singular, used as a substantive, and thus means "to/for one who is willing."

34. *See generally* 65A C.J.S *Assumption of Risk* § 174(1).
35. *Id.*
36. 16 Ariz. App. 583, 494 P.2d 1328 (1972).
37. 494 P.2d 1328, 1330.
38. Prosser and Keeton *supra* note 1, at 485.
39. *Id.* at 471-73.
40. *Id.* at 451-62.
41. *Id.* at 473-74.

CHAPTER NINE

GENERAL TERMS

To be sure, the legal profession has not confined its use of Latin to only discrete subject areas. Many Latin terms transcend fields of law. The words and phrases in this chapter appear in legal writing so frequently and in so many different contexts that all lawyers regularly encounter them. In addition, some of the terms in this chapter are not limited to use in a legal context. Many of the words and phrases have found their way into everyday English use. Others pervade other academic disciplines (especially philosophy).

AD HOC

The phrase *ad hoc* means "for this thing."[1] It is often used in a legal context to mean "for this occasion."

Law professors, casebook authors, and commentators take special delight in accusing courts of making *ad hoc* decisions. An *ad hoc* decision is one which a court makes for the purpose of reaching an equitable result given the specific case in question. *Ad hoc* decisions generally neither rely on precedent nor create a precedent. Such decisions are often said to be "limited to their facts."

The primary fear expressed by the bar about *ad hoc* decisions is they *might* become precedent. Lawyers have long said that "hard cases make bad law."[2] There are cases whose circumstances can create an extremely sympathetic view toward one of the parties. Perhaps an 88-year-old widow is about to lose her home because the bank plans to foreclose. Although the bank may be perfectly within its legal rights to foreclose, we, of course, feel sorry for the widow. In cases like this, it is possible for a judge to find some colorable excuse to decide for the widow and against the bank. This is a "hard case" because the facts present "hard" or sympathetic circumstances. It makes "bad law" because this case now has the potential for creating a precedent concerning the law of foreclosure. The court which decides in favor of the widow has made an *ad hoc* decision. The court may couch its decision in terms of equitable and legally supportable logic, but it is still *ad hoc*.

Courts frequently make *ad hoc* decisions and those decisions are not necessarily bad. However, practicing attorneys and law students alike must be sensitive to and recognize *ad hoc* decisions. The utility of such decisions as precedent is questionable at best.[3]

A FORTIORI

The phrase *a fortiori* literally means "from the more forceful."[4]

A fortiori is a phrase which lawyers have borrowed from philosophers. It is a shorthand way of saying, "if you believed my last argument, you've really got to believe this next one because it is even more compelling, even more forceful."

For example, suppose that you are defending a client accused of robbing a church. According to Pastor Bob's testimony (Pastor Bob is the only eyewitness), he saw the thief leap from the altar, dash out of the side door, and sprint across the church parking lot (a distance of some fifty or sixty yards), all in about six or seven seconds. You introduce evidence showing that even the fastest sprinters on the local college track team had difficulty covering the distance in six or seven seconds. Now you are ready to argue, "Your Honor, if the most fleet-of-foot sprinters on the college track team could barely run the route in question in six or seven seconds, then *a fortiori* my client, who has two bad knees and walks with a limp, certainly could not have been the thief who made off with the money from the collection plate in so swift a manner."

In a case requiring interpretation of a complex question of appeals procedure, Justice Holmes stated, "If express words were thought necessary to save pending appeals, *a fortiori* such words were needed to save appeals not yet taken. . . ."[5]

In short, the phrase *a fortiori* is like a road sign indicating that the writer or speaker is about to present an example or an argument which, in the writer's or speaker's view, is even clearer and stronger than his/her previous example or argument.

DE NOVO

De novo means "from new" or "from afresh."[6]

The phrase *de novo* appears in legal writing most frequently when an author is discussing a *de novo* hearing or a trial *de novo*. Unfortunately the legal system, like all systems and all things human in general, is subject to error. Sometimes an error is so egregious that no amount of procedural patchwork will rectify it. For example, if, during a trial, a juror has done extracurricular investigation on his/her own, or if a judge has misunderstood the applicable law and consequently given the jury instructions which were not in accordance with the law, then the errors involved are so severe that they cannot be alleviated at that particular trial.[7] When judicial or administrative error is sufficiently great, an appellate court or other reviewing entity has the authority to order a *de novo* trial or *de novo* hearing. If, for example, a *de novo* trial is ordered, the litigants start "from new." In other words, the entire trial procedure is begun from scratch because some prejudicial error tainted the previous proceedings.

The concept of *de novo* review can be important in administrative law where a court determines to institute a trial *de novo* rather than merely accepting an agency's finding of fact and reversing on other grounds.[8]

DICTA/DICTUM & RATIO DECIDENDI

Dictum means "a thing which has been said."[9] *Dicta* is simply the plural form of *dictum* and therefore means "things which have been said." The phrase *ratio decidendi*, in the context of the law, means "the ground of deciding."[10] The *ratio decidendi* of a case is the court's explanation for its "holding" in the case.

The holding of a case is the specific legal principle promulgated by the court in its decision. A court might say, "We hold that, because the defendant breached his/her contract with the plaintiff, s/he must pay the plaintiff $10,000, the sum equal to the amount which the plaintiff would have realized had the defendant not breached." This hypothetical *holding* states the rule of expectation damages in contract law and also gives the *ratio decidendi* for that rule.[11]

However, in addition to the holding and *ratio decidendi*, courts generally say other important things in a written opinion. Just because what a court says is not part of the holding of the case or the *ratio decidendi* does not mean that it is unimportant. In legal writing, the things which a court says, which may be important and interesting but neither holding nor *ratio decidendi*, are called *dicta* ("things which have been said").

It is important for law students and practitioners to distinguish between holding, *ratio decidendi*, and *dicta*. The holding and *ratio decidendi* of one court might be precedential but *dicta* can only be influential.[12] The extent to which the *dicta* from one court can influence another court in making its decision depends upon a variety of factors. For example, *dicta* in a U.S. Supreme Court decision will have a great impact upon any court in the land no matter how big, no matter how small. *Dicta* from the New Hampshire Supreme Court will be highly influential in all of the courts in New Hampshire; it might cause another court on any level in the other New England states to think twice; but it probably will have only limited persuasive value in the California Supreme Court.

Recognizing the difference between *dicta*, holding, and *ratio decidendi* is essential in sound legal analysis. Once you have determined whether something a court has said is *dicta, ratio decidendi*, or holding, you then can better evaluate the statement's potential influence in subsequent cases.

PRO FORMA

Pro forma means "according to form."[13]

The phrase *pro forma* typically occurs in law when one tribunal (usually an appellate court) determines that an inferior tribunal, whose decision the principal tribunal is reviewing (usually a lower court), reached its decision in a *pro forma* way. In other words, although the inferior tribunal may have conducted its business using the appropriate procedure, it did not reach its decision rightly on the merits of the matter. Thus, for example, an appellate court may determine that an administrative agency, such as the Federal Reserve Board or the Environmental Protection Agency, decided a case in a *pro forma* manner (i.e., the agency followed proper administrative procedure—"according to form"—but it did not genuinely consider the merits of the case).

Merely because a judge performs a duty in a *pro forma* manner does not necessarily mean that the act is without consequence. *Cramp & Sons Ship & Engine Building Co. v. International Curtiss*

Marine Turbine Co.[14] illustrates the potential significance of *pro forma* conduct by the judiciary. In *Cramp & Sons*, the trial judge, knowing that the case would soon be appealed, entered what he characterized as "a *pro forma* decree, in order to send the controversy to the Court of Appeals as speedily as possible."[15] He added that his decree should "not be construed as affording the slightest intimation of my opinion concerning the merits."[16] He concluded, "I have formed no opinion whatever on that subject. . . . "[17] Later, the trial judge was promoted to the Third Circuit Court of Appeals. When the case came before the Third Circuit he sat on the court to review the case. A federal statute prohibited a judge who passed on a case in the first instance from sitting on the circuit court of appeals for review. The U.S. Supreme Court held that even a *pro forma* decree was sufficient to bar the judge from reviewing the case at the appellate level.[18]

SUA SPONTE

The phrase *sua sponte* is a phrase which occurs often in Latin literature and is probably best translated "of his/her/its/their own volition."[19]

In the context of legal writing, law students and lawyers will probably most often find entities such as courts or administrative agencies doing something *sua sponte* (i.e., of their own volition—without someone else requesting that they act).

Courts *sua sponte* commonly address the question of whether they possess jurisdiction to decide a particular matter. In other words, in cases where neither party questions the court's jurisdiction, the court itself can raise the issue of its own volition. In such cases we say that the court raised the issue of jurisdiction *sua sponte*.[20]

Although courts can, and often do, raise issues other than jurisdiction *sua sponte*, it is useful to remember that, as a general rule, courts are charged with deciding the issues which the litigants properly bring before them.

SUI GENERIS

The phrase *sui generis* means "of its own kind."[21]

A court will sometimes state that a case, problem, or issue is *sui generis*. In other words, in the court's estimation, that case, problem, or issue is unique ("of its own kind"). When a court declares that something is *sui generis*, several important consequences logically flow from that characterization. First, if a court says that a case is *sui generis*, the issues involved are probably issues which have not been decided before by that court: "a case of first impression" for the court. However, in addition, if a court characterizes a case as *sui generis*, the precedential value of the decision will be affected.[22] If a case is truly unique, it is unlikely that many subsequent cases will have similar facts and issues. You will recall that in the case *Edwards v. Lee's Administrator*,[23] Edwards developed a profitable tourist business at his cave, the Great Onyx Cave, which was just a few miles away from the Mammoth Cave in Kentucky. Years later, after the Mammoth Cave had become a national park and the National Park Service had bought out Edwards's business, a neighbor, Lee, claimed that part of the Great Onyx Cave was, in fact, underneath his property. Therefore, Lee sued Edwards for a portion of the profits which he had realized from the Great Onyx Cave.[24] In the first sentence of his concurring opinion, Judge Thomas characterized the case as *sui generis*.[25] Indeed, this is a good example of a case which is *sui generis*. How often will a dispute like this one occur? The unique facts of this case simply are unlikely to arise in litigation on a daily basis.

Cases which are *sui generis* can often elicit *ad hoc* decisions.[26] This only makes sense. If a case presents unique facts and unique issues, it is only logical for the court to render its decision for this occasion only.

■ ENDNOTES

1. The Latin preposition *ad* has many meanings. Here it means "for." *Hoc* is the neuter accusative singular form of the demonstrative pronoun *hic* ("this").

2. *See,* e.g., *Northern Sec. Co. v. United States,* 193 U.S. 197, 400 (1904) (Holmes, J., dissenting).

3. For a discussion of "precedent," *see* Chapter One, *Stare Decisis, supra.*

4. The preposition *a* basically means "from" and can also mean "because of." *Fortiori* is a form of the adjective *fortis* ("strong, powerful, robust, stout"). In particular, *fortiori* is the ablative singular of the comparative form of the adjective *fortis*. Thus, *fortiori* means "stronger" or "more powerful."

5. *Washington Home for Incurables v. American Security & Trust Co.*, 224 U.S. 486, 490 (1911). Justice Holmes's point was simply that if the new law required an express statement of intent to include appeals that were pending at the time that the new law was passed, then an even stronger argument logically follows (*a fortiori*) to support the position that such express language would be required in order for the new law to encompass appeals that were not yet pending when the new law was enacted.

6. The Latin preposition *de* basically means "from." The adjective *novus* means "new, fresh." *Novo* is the ablative singular form of *novus* (the preposition *de* requires that an ablative follow it).

7. *See generally* 5 C.J.S. *Appeal and Error* §§ 1524-35 (1990).

8. *See* Pierce, Shapiro, and Verkuil, Administrative Law and Process § 7.4.1 "De Novo review" at 370-72 (1985).

9. *Dictum* is the perfect passive participle of the Latin verb *dicere* ("to say") in its neuter form.

10. *Ratio* is a Latin noun which has several similar meanings. It can mean "reason, motive, ground," or more specifically "reason brought forward to support a position," and also "theory" or "doctrine." *Decidendi* is the genitive case of the gerund formed from the verb *decidere* (the same verb from which the word *decisis* in the phrase *stare decisis* is derived). *See Stare Decisis*, *supra*, in Chapter One. Among other possible meanings, *decidere* can mean "to bring to a conclusion, to settle, to decide."

11. *See* Restatement (Second) of Contracts, § 357.

12. *See* discussion of "precedent," *supra*, in Chapter I, *Stare Decisis*.

13. The preposition *pro*, in Latin, has several meanings, among which is "according to" or "conformably with." *Forma* means "form, figure, shape" and is here in the ablative case.

14. 228 U.S. 645 (1913).

15. *Id.* at 647.

16. *Id.*

17. *Id.*

18. *Id.* at 649-50.

19. *Sponte* is the ablative singular form of the noun *spons* (the word *spons* itself never actually occurs in Latin literature). *Sponte* means "willingly, voluntarily, of one's own accord, by oneself, unaided." *Sua* is a reflexive adjective describing *sponte* and can mean, according to the particular context, "his own, her own, its own" or "their own."

20. The U.S. Supreme Court has long recognized that it "is obliged to inquire *sua sponte* whenever a doubt arises as to the existence of federal jurisdiction." *Mount Healthy City Dist. Bd. of Educ. v. Doyle*, 429 U.S. 274, 278 (1976) (citations omitted).

21. *Generis* is the genitive singular form of the noun *genus* ("kind, variety, sort") and thus means "of a kind." *Sui* is the genitive form of the Latin reflexive pronoun meaning here "of its own."

22. *See* discussion of "precedent" and *Stare Decisis supra*, in Chapter One.

23. 265 Ky. 418, 96 S.W.2d 1028 (1936). *See* discussion in Chapter Seven, *supra*.

24. He was suing upon the theory of *cujus est solum ejus est usque ad coelum et usque ad inferos*. For a discussion of this Latin phrase and the squabble between Edwards and Lee, *see* Chapter Seven, *supra*.

25. 265 Ky. 418, 429, 96 S.W. 2d 1028, at 1033.

26. See *supra* in this chapter for a more complete discussion of the phrase *ad hoc*.

GLOSSARY

The first item in each entry (in quotation marks) is a translation of the Latin. Those words and phrases which are discussed at greater length in the text are noted with an asterisk [*].

A

A FORTIORI * (General Terms, Constitutional)
"From the more forceful." This phrase indicates that the author of a text believes that the argument which follows is even more clear and powerful than the one which preceded it.

A MENSA ET THORO (Property, Family)
"Away from the table and marriage bed." (Note the classical spelling of *thoro* would have been *toro*, from *torus, tori(m)*. This phrase describes a type of divorce resulting from a separation of husband and wife. Divorce *a mensa et thoro* does not actually extinguish the marriage but instead bars the parties from cohabiting.

A PRIORI (General Terms)
"From that which has preceded." The phrase *a priori* is used in legal writing to indicate that there is a logical connection between one statement and the one which follows. Example: "If defendant, an expert marksman, can hit a 3 × 5 inch target at a distance of 50 meters, then *a priori*, he can hit a 5 × 7 inch target at 40 meters.

A VINCULO MATRIMONII (Property, Family)
"Away from the chain of marriage." Divorce *a vinculo matrimonii* is a complete extinguishing of a marriage.

AB ANTE (General Terms)
"From beforehand." In advance.

AB INITIO* (Contracts, General Terms)

"From the beginning." This phrase is often used to describe the circumstances as they existed at the beginning of a contract (i.e., at the time that parties attempted to create an agreement). If an agreement is void or unenforceable from the beginning, a party who is damaged by the other's failure to perform may still recover at least some damages pursuant to a variety of legal theories (such as unjust enrichment, detrimental reliance, *quantum meruit*, etc.). There are many reasons why a contract may be void, voidable, or otherwise unenforceable *ab initio*. Among the most common reasons are: (1) lack of consideration; (2) absence of a valid offer or acceptance; (3) mistake; (4) the incapacity of one party; (5) duress; (6); material misrepresentation; and (7) public policy.

AB INTESTATO (Property, Wills & Estates)

"From a person who had not made a will." When a person dies, s/he either dies testate (having a valid will) or intestate (without a valid will). The Latin terms describing these possibilities are *ex testamento* and *ab intestato*, respectively. When an individual dies *ab intestato*, the intestate succession laws of the jurisdiction determine disposition of his/her property.

ACTUS NON FACIT REUM, NISI MENS SIT REA (Criminal)

"An act [by itself] does not make a person guilty, unless his/her mind is evil." This phrase expresses the requirement in criminal law that an *actus reus* ("an evil action") alone does not render a person criminally liable; the person must also possess a *mens rea* ("an evil mind") in order to be convicted of a crime.

ACTUS REUS* (Criminal)

"An evil action" An *actus reus* is (are) essentially the external, objective element(s) of a crime, the result of human conduct that the law seeks to prevent. The deed or criminal action that society has chosen to prohibit.

AD DAMNUM (Civil Procedure)

"Towards the attainment of financial loss." The *ad damnum* clause in a complaint or cross complaint is the clause in which the litigant asks the court for money damages.

AD HOC* (General Terms)

"For this thing/for this occasion." Courts make *ad hoc* decisions in order to achieve what they consider just results under the circumstances without necessarily following procedent or a technical interpretation of a statute. Typically, *ad hoc* decisions make poor precedents; hence the maxim: "Hard cases make bad law."

AD LITEM (General Terms)
"For the suit." This Latin term is most commonly found, in a legal context, in the phrase "guardian *ad litem*." A guardian *ad litem* generally protects the interests of a minor (often in proceedings in probate or family court).

AD VALOREM * (Corporations & Tax)
"According to value." Certain things, especially property, are assessed, for tax purposes, *ad valorem*—based on their value.

ADDITUR (Civil Procedure)
"It is added." A court may occasionally determine that a jury's award is too small. On such occasions, the court may award an *additur*, i.e., a sum of money over and above the damages awarded by the jury.

ADEMPTIO (Property, Wills & Estates)
"A revocation of a legacy." If a person's will provides that his/her gold watch should go to his/her nephew, Jonathan, and, as it turns out, the deceased actually sold the gold watch two years before death, courts generally hold that the gift of the gold watch fails by *ademptio*, or, in its anglicized form, "ademption."

ALEA[TORY PROMISE, CONTRACT] * (Contracts)
"A contract like a game of chance." The English adjective "aleatory" derives from the Latin noun *alea* ("a game of dice, a game of chance"). An aleatory contract is a contract where the performance of at least one of the parties is contingent upon the occurrence of a fortuitous event. Insurance contracts are the most common legal aleatory contracts since the insurance company's payment to the insured or the insured's beneficiary is contingent upon some fortuitous (often catastrophic) event (e.g., fire, theft, flood, death, etc.).

ALIAS (Criminal)
"On other occasions." When a person uses a name that is different from his/her legal name, we say that the name s/he uses on those other occasions (i.e., at times other than when s/he uses his/her own name) is an *alias*.

ALTER EGO * (Corporations & Tax)

"A second I, a second self." Most jurisdictions recognize that a corporate promoter can act as a second self for the nascent corporation. Additionally, under certain circumstances, when corporate officers or directors engage in fraud or other culpable conduct, courts may "pierce the corporate veil" and hold that the corporation is merely the *alter ego* of the officers or directors. When a court "pierces the corporate veil," the officers or directors can be held personally liable.

AMBIGUITAS CONTRA STIPULATOREM EST (Contracts)

"An ambiguity is [construed] against the drafter." This canon of contract construction articulates the notion that an ambiguous word, phrase, sentence, etc., should be interpreted most favorably in favor of the non-drafting party (i.e., construed against the drafter).

AMBIGUUM PACTUM CONTRA VENDITOREM INTERPRETANDUM EST (Contracts)

"An ambiguous agreement must be interpreted against the seller." This notion is based upon the theory that a seller usually controls the terms of an agreement and usually drafts the contract. *See also "Ambiguitas contra stipulatorem est," supra.*

AMICUS CURIAE * (Constitutional)

"A friend of the court." A non-party often submits an *amicus curiae* brief in order to apprise the court of its (the non-party's) position in a case. The U.S. government, which frequently has a stake in the outcome of federal cases, often submits *amicus curiae* briefs.

ANIMUS CONTRAHENDI (Contracts)

"A mind to contract." Before the modern acceptance of the objective theory of contract law, it was traditionally believed that a person, in order to be held liable under the terms of a contract, had first to intend subjectively to be bound by the contract (i.e., the person had to intend to form a contract). The objective theory of contract law suggests that a party must *manifest* an *animus contrahendi* as a condition precedent to being bound by a contract.

ANIMUS DONANDI (Property)

"A mind to give." A donor of property must manifest an intent to transfer the property in question; s/he must have an *animus donandi* (i.e., an intention to transfer).

ANIMUS FURANDI (Criminal)

"A mind to steal." A dimension of the *mens rea* which is required for theft is an *animus furandi*. A defendant must possess (and thus be capable of possessing) a criminal intent to appropriate the property of another in order to be found criminally liable for theft.

ANIMUS REVOCANDI (Contracts)

"A mind to revoke." In order to effectively revoke an offer, an offeror must manifest an intent to revoke (i.e., an *animus revocandi*) to the offeree.

ANIMUS TESTANDI (Property, Wills & Estates)

"A mind to make a will." One of the cardinal rules of the law of wills is that the person making the will (the testator or testatrix) must actually intend to have the document that s/he is signing function as a will. Lawyers generally call this state of mind to make a will "testamentary intent" or an *"animus testandi."*

AQUA CEDIT SOLO (Property)

"Water passes into possession because of the land." When land is sold, the title to the water on that land passes along with it.

AQUA CURRIT ET DEBET CURRERE UT CURRERE SOLEBAT (Property)

"Water runs and ought to run as it was accustomed to run." Riparian owners ordinarily expect to be able to use the water courses that flow through their land. An upstream owner cannot unreasonably interfere with the downstream owner's use of water.

ARGUENDO (General Terms)

"For the sake of argument." Lawyers and judges use this philosophical term in legal writing when they do not necessarily wish to concede a point but offer, hypothetically, to consider the consequences which would flow from an argument if the point at issue were true.

ARGUMENTUM A CONTRARIO (General Terms)

"An argument from the opposite [view]." This phrase is found in legal writing indicating that the argument which follows presents a view directly opposite from the one which the writer has just expressed.

ARGUMENTUM A SIMILI VALET IN LEGE (General Terms)

"Argument by analogy governs in law."

ARGUMENTUM AB AUCTORITATE EST FORTISSIMUM IN LEGE (General Terms)
"Argument from authority/precedent is the most forceful in law."

ARGUMENTUM AD HOMINEM (General Terms)
"Argument against the individual." An attack on the qualities of the individual rather than the merits of the controversy. Arguments of this nature are virtually useless in law.

ASSUMPSIT* (General Terms, Contracts)
"S/he/it promised." At common law an action in contracts typically used to allege that another party has not fulfilled his/her/its promise under the terms of a contract.

AUDITA QUERELA (Criminal, Civil Procedure)
"A complaint that has been heard." A defendant uses a writ of *audita querela* when judgment has been entered against him/her and the defendant then seeks to open the judgment because s/he (the defendant) has subsequently learned information that s/he could have used as a defense.

B

BONA FIDES * (General Terms, Contracts)
"Good faith." The phrase *bona fides* is typically used in legal writing to describe the honesty required of parties who contract.

C

CAPIAS (Civil Procedure)
"You may seize." At common law *capias* was the name given to certain writs both before and after judgment.

CAVEAT (General Terms)
"Let him/her/it beware." Legal writers sometimes use the word *caveat* by itself to mean "warning." In such instances *caveat* means that the statement that the writer has made may not always be true. The explanation that follows then ordinarily illustrates the potential flaw or exception in the writer's conclusion or analysis.

CAVEAT EMPTOR * (Contracts, Torts)
"Let the buyer beware." This Latin phrase expresses the notion that buyers have a duty to carefully inspect goods before purchasing them. Modern consumer laws, unfair trade practices laws, and product liability laws have mitigated the doctrine of *caveat emptor*.

CAVEAT VENDITOR (Contracts, Torts)
"Let the seller beware." This Latin phrase expresses the awareness that sellers are subject to a number of implied warranties (e.g., warranty of title and warranty of merchantability) under the Uniform Commercial Code as well as the doctrine of products liability.

CERTIORARI * (Constitutional, Civil Procedure)
"To be made more certain, to be apprised." Unless the U.S. Supreme Court is required by either 28 U.S.C. § 1257 or 28 U.S.C. § 1254 to take a case on appeal, a party seeking Supreme Court review must apply for a grant of *certiorari*. Four Supreme Court Justices must decide that a case is sufficiently important before the Court will grant *certiorari*. Although *certiorari* is entirely discretionary, the Supreme Court typically grants *certiorari* when two or more federal courts of appeal have reached conflicting conclusions on the same issue, or when the supreme courts of two or more states have reached conflicting conclusions on the same issue.

CESSANTE RATIONE, CESSAT ETIAM LEX (General Terms)
"After the [underlying] rationale has ceased, the law also ceases." This maxim explains one reason why courts overrule old cases. When the circumstances which created a need for a particular law no longer exist, that law itself no longer has reason to exist either.

CHIROGRAPHUM APUD DEBITOREM REPERTUM PRAESUMITUR SOLUTUM (Contracts)
"A bond discovered in the custody of the debtor is assumed to have been paid." Generally, a creditor retains possession of an instrument that is evidence of a debt (e.g., a bond, deed, etc.). Customarily, when the debtor has paid the debt, the creditor transfers the debt instrument to the debtor. Therefore, if the debtor has the debt instrument in his/her possession, Anglo-American legal custom creates the presumption that s/he (the debtor) has paid the debt in full.

COGNOVIT (Contracts)
"S/he realized." The clause in a contract wherein one party (typically the buyer) agrees to consent to jurisdiction in the state where the

seller resides is called a *cognovit* clause. Of course buyers are more likely to default if they are forced to travel great distances to contest a suit. In cases involving consumer transactions, most states now consider *cognovit* clauses invalid (especially where the contract is an adhesion contract).

COLLOQUIUM (Torts)
"Talk, conversation." In the law of defamation, the plaintiff's allegation that at least one person reasonably interpreted the defendant's statement to have referred to him/her (the plaintiff) is called the *colloquium*. In other words, *colloquium* refers to the transmission of a defamatory statement to a third party.

CONCORDARE LEGES LEGIBUS EST OPTIMUS INTERPAETANDI MODUS (General Terms)
"The best method of construction is to harmonize [some] laws with [other] laws." A basic principle of American jurisprudence is the notion that laws should be consistent. Therefore, judges endeavor to construe different statutes, regulations, and the like in such a way that they do not conflict with one another. *See also In Pari Materia, infra.*

CONSORTIUM * (Torts)
"Partnership, equal share." The spouse of an accident victim may sue a tortfeasor for loss of *consortium* (i.e., loss of companionship, services, etc.). Suits brought by parents whose children have been injured and vice-versa are also loss of *consortium* claims; the chances of recovery in the parent/child and child/parent cases are presently uncertain.

CONTRA BONOS MORES (General Terms)
"Contrary to sound established practices."

CONTRA PROFERENTEM (Contracts, General Terms)
"Against the one who produces." In general, ambiguities in documents are construed against the drafter. This canon of construction relies on the assumption that a person who produces a document has the capability to avoid ambiguities when drafting it.

CORAM NON JUDICE (Constitutional)
"In the presence of one who is not a judge." If a court, without appropriate jurisdiction, nevertheless renders a decision in a case, the decision is said to be void because it was tried *coram non judice*

(i.e., before a person who wasn't really a judge because s/he lacked jurisdiction).

CORPUS DELECTI (Criminal, Torts)
"The body/structure/framework of the misconduct/crime." Lawyers typically use this term to refer to the physical object of a crime such as a murder victim's body.

CORPUS JURIS (General Terms)
"A body/compendium of law." The most famous *corpus juris* is clearly the *Corpus Juris Civilis* of Justinian published in 533 A.D. Today most lawyers know this phrase because of West Publishing Company's comprehensive multivolume encyclopedia, *Corpus Juris Secundum* ("C.J.S"), "The Second Compendium of Law."

CRIMEN FALSI * (Evidence)
"A crime of falsehood." One way to impeach a witness's credibility is by introducing evidence showing that the witness has been convicted of a crime that involves dishonesty or false statement, such as perjury, fraud, bribery, etc. Such crimes of dishonesty are frequently referred to as *crimen falsi*.

CUI BONO (General Terms)
"For whose benefit."

CUJUS EST SOLUM EJUS EST USQUE AD COELUM ET USQUE AD INFEROS * (Property)
"Whose land it is, is his/hers all the way to the sky (Heaven) and all the way to the lower world (Hell)." This Latin maxim expresses the ancient notion of property law, which holds that an owner of real property, in addition to owning the surface of the land, also owns all of the airspace extending directly above the surface (without limit) and also everything under the surface (presumably all the way down to the center of the earth where the landowner on the opposite side of the globe takes over).

 D

DAMNUM ABSQUE INJURIA * (Torts)
"Injury without wrong." If a person causes harm to another while doing a lawful act or while exercising a legal right, or doing that which

the law authorizes him/her to do (in a lawful manner), such damage is not actionable.

DEBITA SEQUUNTUR PERSONAM DEBITORIS

"Debts follow the actual being of the debtor." This phrase provides a rationale for determining *in rem* jurisdiction when the *res* is a movable property. This is also the holding of *Harris v. Balk*, 198 U.S. 215 (1905). The theory has been severely criticized on several grounds. *See generally* F. James, Jr and G. Hazard, Jr., Civil Procedure 83-85 (1985).

DE BONIS ASPORTATIS (Criminal)

"Concerning goods that have been carried away." An action against a trespasser who is accused of having stolen goods.

DE FACTO * (Constitutional, General Terms)

"From that which has been done." If something—for example, racial discrimination or the denial of any constitutional right—occurs inadvertently, without a conscious plan, it is said to happen *de facto*.

DE MINIMIS NON CURAT LEX (General Terms)

"The law does not concern itself about trivial matters." This maxim expresses the notion that allows judicial and prosecutorial discretion when it is determined that, in the interests of efficiency, it is best to ignore insignificant breaches of law.

DE JURE * (Constitutional, General Terms)

"From the law." When something—for example, racial discrimination or the denial of any constitutional right—occurs through a purposeful, planned process (e.g., by some lawmaking or rulemaking authority), it is said to happen *de jure*.

DE NOVO * (General Terms, Civil Procedure, Constitutional)

"From anew." When a *de novo* proceeding is ordered or permitted, the parties begin from scratch; as if the earlier proceeding had never occurred. Under certain circumstances a party is entitled to a hearing or trial *de novo* (e.g., in many states a party who is displeased with a decision from a probate judge regarding certain matters is entitled to a *de novo* trial in the state's trial court).

DEVASTAVIT (Property)

"S/he has laid to waste." When a person holds less than a fee simple estate (e.g., a life estate), s/he is liable to those persons to whom the estate will later pass for any damage to the estate caused either intentionally or by neglect. When such a person damages the estate, the Latin phrase used to describe the injury is *devastavit*. This principle applies to trustees of estates as well.

DICTUM/DICTA * (General Terms, Constitutional)
"A thing which has been said/Things which have been said." When a court makes important statements concerning important issues (but which are neither the holding of the case nor the *ratio decidendi*), those statements are called *dicta*.

DOLI CAPAX (Criminal)
"Capable of an unlawful act." In modern criminal law this phrase is the equivalent of the M'Naughten Rule (i.e., the common law test for insanity that asks whether the defendant knew that what s/he was doing was wrong).

DONATIO CAUSA MORTIS * (Property)
"A gift by reason of death." When a donor makes a gift to another person because s/he (the donor) thinks that death is imminent, certain legal consequences ensue. In order for a *donatio causa mortis* to be valid, the following events must occur: (1) the donor must be in such a condition that his/her death is imminent; (2) the donor must deliver the gift to the donee; (3) the donor must intend the gift to become effective only upon his/her death; and (4) the donor must die (without remission) as a result of the condition mentioned above.

DUM CASTA VIXERIT (Property, Family)
"For as long as s/he lives chaste." Some divorce and separation agreements contain a provision that requires one spouse (traditionally the husband) to support the other (traditionally the wife) until the latter had sex with a third party (or as a practical matter—until the spouse being supported remarried).

■ E

EJUSDEM GENERIS (General Terms)
"Of identical classification." This canon of construction holds that when a statute lists a specific group of items and then concludes with a catchall characterization of those items, courts should construe the catchall phrase to encompass only things that are "of identical classification" with the specific list enumerated.

ET AEQUO ET BONO (General Terms)

"From both the equitable and the good." Law generally strives to achieve that which is both equitable and good under the circumstances. Courts strive to decide cases based upon reasons which are *et aequo et bono.*

ET AL. (ET ALIA) (General Terms)

"And others." When a case involves more than one party as a plaintiff or more than one party as a defendant, rather than listing all of the named parties, legal writers simply write the first named party and then use the abbreviation *et al.* to refer to the other plaintiffs or defendants. However, A Uniform System of Citation (the "Blue Book") provides that, in textual sentences, one should omit the abbreviation *et al. See* A Uniform System of Citation, Rule 10.2.1(a) A p. 57.

ET SEQ. (ET SEQUITUR) (General Terms)

"And that which follows." Legal writers often use the abbreviation *et seq.* to refer to pages in a volume or to statutes. For example, the U.S. Copyright Act is 17 U.S.C. § 101 *et seq.* That is, §101 of Title 17 of the United States Code and then §§ 102, 103, 104, *etc.* (the statute sections that follow § 101).

EX CONTRACTU (Contract)

"Out of contract." This phrase refers to the rights and obligations which arise from a valid and enforceable contract.

EX PARTE (General Terms, Constitutional)

"From the party." A proceeding is *ex parte* when it is conducted in a non-adversarial forum on behalf of one party only. When a case is entitled "*Ex Parte* _____ ," the named party is the one who has applied to have the case heard.

EX POST FACTO * (Criminal, Constitutional)

"From after that which was done." A criminal law which renders an action done before the passing of the law criminal, and which was innocent when done, is unconstitutional because it is *ex post facto.* Other examples of unconstitutional *ex post facto* laws are those which: (1) increase the punishment for a crime already committed; (2) make an act a more serious type of crime than when it was committed; and (3) alter the legal rules of evidence in such a way that the proof required to convict the offender is less than when the crime was committed.

EX PROPRIO VIGORE (Constitutional)

"From one's own strength." This phrase means essentially the same thing as *sua sponte* (*see infra*). When a court does something *ex proprio vigore*, it does so on its own initiative.

EX TEMPORE (General Terms)

"From time." Legal writers use the phrase *ex tempore* in two distinct ways. *Ex tempore* can mean "because of time considerations" or "on the spot" (i.e., unprepared).

EX TESTAMENTO (Property, Wills & Estates)

"From one who has made a will." When a person dies, s/he either dies testate (having a valid will) or intestate (without a valid will). The Latin terms describing these possibilities are *ex testamento* and *ab intestato*, respectively. When an individual dies *ex testamento*, his/her executor/executrix disposes of the estate in accordance with the provisions of the will.

EX VI TERMINI (General Terms, Contracts)

"From the strength of the remotest limit." When a legal document or statute can be construed on its own, without referring to other sources, we say that we can construe it *ex vi termini* (i.e., from the meaning evidenced by what the document or statute itself says). This is essentially the same as declaring that the meaning is clear from "the four corners" of the document.

■ F

FACTUM PROBANDUM (Evidence)

"A fact that must be proved." In litigation, the moving party must prove (usually by a preponderance of the evidence in civil cases and beyond a reasonable doubt in criminal matters) certain facts in order to meet the technical burden of production/proof at trial. A fact that a party must prove to fulfill this burden is a *factum probandum*.

FALSUS IN UNO, FALSUS IN OMNIBUS* (Evidence)

"Deceitful/lying in one instance, [therefore] deceitful/lying in all." Litigators may attempt to impeach a witness's testimony by showing that s/he (the witness) has lied about one thing, and consequently (so the argument goes), the witness is likely to lie about everything. Under modern rules of evidence, the *falsus in uno* doctrine has relatively little opportunity to succeed because court rules generally prohibit the introduction of extrinsic evidence (i.e., evidence that is collateral or not directly relevant to an issue before the court) to attack a witness's credibility. *See* e.g., Fed. R. Evid. § 608.

FERAE NATURAE (Property, Torts)
"Wild animals of nature." Wild animals provide provocative subject matter for property and tort problems (especially in law school). In property class the question is generally, "Who owns a wild animal?" In torts the question generally is, "Who is responsible for injuries caused by the animal?" Depending upon the facts, the answers can vary. Landowners are generally considered to own the wild animals in or on their real estate by title *ratione soli* (*see Ratione Soli, infra*).

FORUM NON CONVENIENS * (Civil Procedure)
"An inconvenient place for conducting judicial business." A defendant, for one reason or another, may prefer not to defend a suit in the jurisdiction selected by the plaintiff. S/he may argue that the forum is inconvenient because most of the witnesses live in another forum (i.e., typically another state), because most of the material evidence is in another forum, etc. If the court sees fit, it may dismiss the case on the grounds of *forum non conveniens*. In such instances, the plaintiff is forced to start again in another, presumably more convenient, forum. Among federal district courts, cases are transferred rather than dismissed and begun anew.

FRACTIONEM DIEI NON RECIPIT LEX (General Terms)
"Law does not count a fraction of a day as allowable." As a general rule of construction, statutes and legal documents take effect without regard to portions of a day. For example, if a girl was born at 3:37 A.M. on May 29, 1986, the law will regard her as 21 years old at a nanosecond after midnight on May 29, 2007. She will not have to wait until 3:37 A.M. to be considered 21 years old as far as the law is concerned.

FRAUS EST CELARE FRAUDEM (Criminal, General Terms)
"To conceal a fraud is fraud."

G

GRATIS (General Terms)
"Without payment" (i.e., for free). Services that lawyers provide *pro bono* are also *gratis.*

H

HABEAS CORPUS * (Criminal, Constitutional)
"You may retain the body." *Habeas corpus* is an extraordinary remedy by which a prisoner petitions, typically, a federal court for a writ of *habeas corpus*, thereby asking the court to review the constitutionality of his/her incarceration resulting from a criminal conviction in a lower (often state) court.

HABENDUM (Property)
"That which must be held." The *habendum* clause in a real property deed is the clause usually containing the words "to have and to hold." This clause used to be the most important part of a real property deed. The *habendum* clause indicates what kind of estate the grantee takes (e.g., fee simple absolute, fee simple determinable, life estate, etc.).

I

I.E. (ID EST) (General Terms)
"It is." Legal writers use the abbreviation "i.e." to tell the reader that what follows is an explanation of what they (the writers) had just stated.

IBID. (IBIDEM) (General Terms)
"In that very place to which one's attention has already been drawn." A Uniform System of Citation does not officially recognize *ibid.* as a citation form. Nevertheless, some legal writers use the abbreviation *ibid.* interchangeably with *id.* to indicate to the reader that a particular reference is precisely the same as the one that s/he (the writer) had referred to previously. *See Id. (Idem), infra.*

ID. (IDEM) (General Terms)
"The same, identical with that previously mentioned." Legal writers use the abbreviation *id.* to indicate that a cited reference is precisely the same as the one immediately before it. *See* A Uniform System of Citation, Rule 4.1, p. 40.

IMMOBILIA SITUM SEQUUNTUR (Property)
"Immovable things go with [their] site." Property law generally presumes that structures, fixtures, and other immovable property (e.g., crops) pass when the land upon which those things are located is sold.

IMPOSSIBILIUM NULLA OBLIGATIO EST (Contracts, General Terms)
"That which is impossible is no legal obligation."

IN ARTICULO MORTIS (General Terms, Property, Criminal)
"In the moment of death."

IN CAMERA (General Terms)
"In the room." We refer to proceedings *in camera* when they are held in the judge's chambers (i.e., in the judge's room). *In camera* proceedings exclude non-party spectators (e.g., the press).

IN CONTRACTIS TACITE INSUNT QUAE SUNT MORIS ET CONSUETUDINIS (Contracts)
"Things that are matters of custom and habitual course of dealing are tacitly present in legal agreements/contracts."

IN CRIMINALIBUS, PROBATIONE DEBENT ESSE LUCE CLARIORES (Criminal)
"In criminal proceedings the things which establish proof ought to be clearer than the light of day." American jurisprudence generally requires that proof in criminal cases be "beyond a reasonable doubt."

IN EXTREMIS (General Terms, Property, Criminal)
"In the final stages [of life]." Acts done *in extremis* are those done shortly before death. For example, a gift *causa mortis* is, by definition, done while the donor is *in extremis*. The same is true regarding the so-called "dying declaration" exception to the hearsay rule of evidence.

IN FLAGRANTE DELICTO (Criminal, Torts)
"In the offense [as it is] burning," i.e., at the very moment that an offense is committed.

IN FORMA PAUPERIS (Civil Procedure, Criminal, Constitutional) "In the procedure of a poor man." When a plaintiff (or appellant in the case of an appeal) believes that s/he does not have financial resources necessary to pay for filing fees and other incidental court costs, s/he (the plaintiff/appellant) generally can ask the court to waive those fees by proceeding *in forma pauperis*.

IN FUTURO (General Terms)
"In the future."

IN JURE NON REMOTA CAUSA, SED PROXIMA SPECTATUR (Torts)
"In law it is not a remote cause, but the proximate cause that is looked to." This Latin maxim expresses one of the most difficult and important concepts in the law of negligence and torts: proximate cause. For example, merely because a gas station attendant was slow filling a gas tank, and his/her delay caused a driver to arrive at an intersection 10 minutes later than s/he (the driver) would have otherwise, the attendant's conduct would not be considered the proximate cause of an accident which occurred at the intersection. The negligence of the driver who caused the accident itself would, more than likely, be the proximate cause, not the slothful attendant.

IN LIMINE* (Evidence, General Terms)
"On the threshold (doorway)." This phrase is generally found in the legal term "motion in limine." A motion in limine is a motion which an attorney makes at the beginning of a trial, for example, requesting that certain matters (e. g., certain questions) be excluded during the proceedings lest they prejudice the jury.

IN LOCO PARENTIS (Torts)
"In place of the parent." Certain institutions (e. g., a boarding school) may, under certain circumstances, assume the duties owed to a minor by a parent. In such cases the institution is said to be acting *in loco parentis*.

IN MEDIAS RES (General Terms)
"In the middle of things."

IN PARI DELICTO (Contracts and Torts)
"In equal fault." This phrase refers to a situation in which two or more persons share blame equally. In a tort context this refers to the notion of joint and several liability.

IN PARI MATERIA (General Terms)

"In subject matter corresponding in function." This canon of statutory construction tells us that statutes should be "read together." In other words, we should interpret statutes consistently with one another.

IN PERSONAM * (Civil Procedure)

"Against the person." *In personam* jurisdiction is jurisdiction which a court possesses over an individual (or a corporate entity) based primarily upon that individual's (or entity's) physical presence within the boundaries of the forum. A person's domicile (i.e., the place where a person lives and intends to remain indefinitely) also generally bestows *in personam* jurisdiction on a court. Personal jurisdiction can also be based on consent, long-arm statutes, and conducting business within the state.

IN PRAESENTI (General Terms)

"In the present."

IN RE (Civil Procedure, General Terms)

"In the matter." Cases which involve property (i.e., things, not adversarial parties), such as some probate proceedings, are often titled *In Re _____* .

IN REM * (Civil Procedure, Property)

"Against the thing." *In rem* jurisdiction is based upon a court's ability to exercise its authority over a thing, not a person. Some scholars contend that foreclosure on real estate and quiet title actions are *in rem*. Others maintain that the only pure *in rem* actions are those relating to probate, bankruptcy, escheat, or divorce.

IN TERROREM (Contracts, Property)

"Into fear." An *in terrorem* clause is a clause which lawyers often put into a lease or a will to frighten the lessee or legatee into conforming his/her conduct in accordance with the desires of the drafter's client. For example, a testator might provide that a legatee's legacy will lapse if s/he contests the will. Such a clause is intended to deter the legatee from contesting the will.

IN UTERO (Criminal, Constitutional, Wills & Estates, General Terms)

"In the womb." Lawyers use the phrase *in utero* in a variety of contexts. For example, the phrase often appears in a criminal/constitutional context to refer to a fetus (in an abortion-rights case). In the law of wills, most jurisdictions presume that a legacy intended for "all children" includes all children *in utero* at the time of the *testator's/testatrix's* death as well.

INFRA (General Terms)

"Below, underneath." Legal writers use the word *infra* to indicate that the preceding reference appears later (i.e., below) in the text or notes.

INJURIA SERVI DOMINUM PERTINGIT (Torts)

"A servant's unlawful conduct reaches/extends to [his/her] master." This maxim essentially restates the notion of *respondeat superior*. *See generally* Restatement (Second) of Agency § 219. Also see *Respondeat Superior, infra.*

INTER ALIA (General Terms)

"Among other things." Legal writers often say, "The court, *inter alia*, stated x, y, & z." In other words, the court said several things, but it also said the specific thing which the author is presenting.

INTER PARTES (Civil Procedure, General Terms)

"Between parties." *Inter partes* proceedings are contrasted with *ex parte* proceedings. For example, when an applicant seeks trademark registration with the U.S. Patent and Trademark Office, the procedure is initially *ex parte* (i.e., the applicant tries to convince the government that the mark is registrable without having another party in an adversarial posture). However, after the trademark-examining attorney has determined that the mark is registrable, it is possible for anyone who believes that registration of the mark might injure them to initiate an *inter partes* proceeding against the applicant in an attempt to prevent registration (this procedure is called "opposition").

INTER[STATE] * (Constitutional)

"Between, or among, states." Activity which involves two or more states is interstate activity. If such activity falls within the definition of "commerce," Congress has the power to regulate it under the Commerce Clause of the Constitution (which affects interstate commerce).

INTER VIVOS * (Property)

"Among the living." When a property transfer is made *inter vivos*, in order to be valid the donor must manifest an intent to transfer the gift to another person (the "donee"), the donor must deliver the gift to the donee, and the donee must accept the gift.

INTRA[STATE] * (Constitutional)
"Within a state." Activity which is confined solely within a state's borders is intrastate activity. Such activity (which is difficult to isolate in today's society), even if it constitutes "commerce," cannot be subject to regulation by Congress under the Constitution's Commerce Clause (because the Commerce Clause affects only interstate commerce).

IPSE DIXIT (General Terms)
"He, himself, said [it]." When, for example, a judge states a legal principle without referring to any precedent or authority for that principle, legal writers might comment that the judge made the statement *ipse dixit* (i.e., with no authority but because he, himself, offered the proposition).

IPSO FACTO (General Terms)
"By means of that which has been done itself." If something is accomplished *ipso facto*, it is accomplished solely by the doing. For example, the decision in case B might *ipso facto* overrule case A (even though case B does not expressly state that it is overruling or even intends to overrule case A).

IPSO JURE (General Terms)
"Because of the law itself."

■ J

JUDEX A QUO (Civil Procedure)
"The judge from whom." When a case is appealed to a higher court, the judge (or court) whose opinion is being appealed is referred to as the *judex a quo*.

JUDEX AD QUEM (Civil Procedure)
"The judge to whom." When a case is appealed to a higher court, a judge (or court) to whom the case is appealed is called the *judex ad quem*.

JUDEX AEQUITATEM SEMPER SPECTARE DEBET (General Terms)
"A judge ought to always consider equity."

JUDEX DEBET JUDICARE SECUNDUM ALLEGATA ET PROBATA (Evidence)
"A judge ought to decide cases in accordance with matters that were alleged and proven."

JUDEX NON POTEST ESSE TESTIS IN PROPRIA CAUSA (Evidence)
"A judge is unable to be a witness in his/her own case." Fed. R. Evid. 605 provides that "[t]he judge presiding at the trial may not testify in that trial as a witness. No objection need be made in order to preserve the point."

JURA PUBLICA ANTEFERENDA PRIVATIS (General Terms)
"Public rights must be given precedence over private [rights]."

JURAT (General Terms)
"S/he swears/takes an oath/affirms/declares." The clause in a will, contract, application, or other legal document where the person who is about to sign makes a written statement in the form of an oath is called the *jurat*. A *jurat* often begins with words like "I solemnly swear that. . . . "

JURATORES SUNT JUDICES FACTI (Civil Procedure)
"Jurors are the judges of fact." In a typical jury trial, the judge determines matters of law and the jury determines what the facts of the case are.

JURE UXORIS (Property)
"By right of the wife." In traditional English common law, a husband acquired whatever estate his wife owned when she married him. When the first child was born in the marriage, the estate *jure uxoris* merged into the husband's estate by the custom called "curtesy." Most states in the U.S. today have abolished the estate *jure uxoris* by statute. Thus, a married woman in most states in the U.S. controls her own property.

JUS (General Terms)
"Law; a legal system or code; a court, a right." As a general (although not immutable) rule, the word *jus* has a more abstract meaning than *lex. See Lex, infra.*

JUS ACCRESCENDI (Property)
"The right of that which must accrue." This is the Latin phrase which has come to be equated with the right of survivorship created

by joint tenancy. When a joint tenant dies, the deceased joint tenant's interest immediately accrues to the other joint tenant(s) by the *jus accrescendi* (i.e., right of survivorship). Most jurisdictions today favor tenancy in common (i.e., with no right of survivorship) to joint tenancy.

JUS CIVILE (General Terms)
"The law of and for citizens; civil law."

JUS COMMUNE (General Terms)
"The common law; law affecting the whole community or state." In Anglo-American law, the common law is the judge-made law derived from cases (i.e., law derived through custom, not from a code or statute).

JUS GENTIUM (General Terms)
"The law of nations." The *jus gentium* is the law which is universally accepted. In today's world, it is questionable whether the laws which have traditionally been considered *jura gentium* should still be so acknowledged.

JUS NATURALE (General Terms)
"Natural law." *Jus naturale* has traditionally been the law applicable to all people at all times, the universally acknowledged principles of law which exist due to the nature of our world.

JUS PRIVATUM (General Terms)
"The law of or relating to a private person or a person in his/her private capacity."

JUS PUBLICUM (General Terms)
"The law of the people; the law authorized, provided, or maintained by the state."

JUS TERTII * (Property)
"The right of a third party." A defendant raises the *jus tertii* defense when s/he has possession of property which a plaintiff claims rightfully belongs to him/her (the plaintiff). The defendant claims that, although s/he may not actually own the property, the plaintiff does not own it either. Rather, the defendant claims that some unknown third party owns the property. Therefore, the defendant asserts that s/he has a better claim to the property in question than does the plaintiff. More often than not, this defense fails (especially when the

plaintiff shows that s/he had prior peaceable possession of the property).

▪ L

LAESIO ENORMIS (Contracts)
"An irregular (or very large) injury." *Laesio enormis* was an ancient and medieval doctrine by which courts possessed the power and authority to provide relief to a party to a contract who had made what was essentially a very poor deal. For example, if one person agreed to exchange a prosperous farm in return for a small sack of meal, it is clear that, from an objective standpoint, the farm is far more valuable than the small sack of meal. In such circumstances, under the doctrine of *laesio enormis* (which is based upon a theory of objective value), a court would be capable of providing relief for the party who had "given away" the family farm.

LEGES VIGILANTIBUS, NON DORMIENTIBUS, SUBSERVIUNT (Property, General Terms)
"Laws lend support to those who are vigilant, not to those who are sleeping." Generally laws protect those who actively maintain their property and their rights. For example, the doctrine of adverse possession protects those who look after their real estate but it does not protect those who abandon their property and fail to watch over their land (i.e., those who are sleeping).

LEONIANA SOCIETAS (Corporations & Tax)
"A lion's partnership (i.e., a partnership in which one partner takes the lion's share)."

LEX
"The law; the legal machinery of the state; a statute; a constitution; a legal right; an ordinance; a regulation; a principle." As a general (although not immutable) rule, the word "*lex*" has a more concrete meaning than "*jus.*"

LEX FORI (Torts, Civil Procedure, Conflicts)
"The law of the court." One traditional notion in the field of conflict of laws is that, as a general rule, the law of the place where a case is tried (i.e., the court or forum) should govern the case.

LEX LOCI CONTRACTUS (Contracts, Civil Procedure, Conflicts)
"The law of the place of the contract." In the field of conflicts of law, a traditional approach in contracts cases is to apply the law of the jurisdiction where the contract was formed.

LEX LOCI DELICTUS (Torts, Civil Procedure, Conflicts)
"The law of the place of the wrongful conduct." In the field of conflicts of law, a traditional approach in torts cases is to apply the law of the jurisdiction where the tort occurred.

LEX LOCI REI SITAE (Property, Civil Procedure, Conflicts)
"The law of the place of the property having been built/situated." As a general rule, the law of the jurisdiction where property is located governs the disposition of that property.

LEX PROSPICIT, NON RESPICIT (General Terms)
"The law looks forward, not backward." Generally laws are deemed to operate prospectively. Occasionally legislatures enact civil laws with the intent that they will have a retroactive effect but such instances are the exception, not the rule. The U.S. Constitution prohibits criminal laws from acting retroactively. *See Ex Post Facto, supra.*

LEX TALIONIS (General Terms, Criminal Law)
"The law of exacting compensation in kind." In the Bible and several legal codes from the ancient Near East (e.g., the Code of Hammurabi, c. 1750 B.C.) a number of laws are said to be *leges talionis* because the punishment for the crime committed is the precise mirror image of the crime itself. For example, Law No. 197 in the Code of Hammurabi provides: "If he [an *awelum*, i.e., a free man of the noble class] has broken the bone of another *awelum*, they shall break his bone."

LINEA RECTA SEMPER PRAEFERTUR TRANSVERSALI
(Property, Wills, Estates)
"A direct line of ancestry is always given priority over one from the side (i.e., a collateral one)."

LIS (General Terms)
"A dispute at law, a lawsuit."

LIS PENDENS (Civil Procedure, General Terms)
"A lawsuit hanging/a lawsuit being undetermined/a lawsuit that is still 'up in the air.'" A notice of *lis pendens* is filed in order to inform the public when a lawsuit is pending that could affect title to property.

LOCUS POENITENTIAE (Contracts)

"A place [in time] of repenting." When a party to an illegal contract (e.g., a gambling contract) desires to get out of it before the contract's illegal purpose is achieved, the law grants him/her a *locus poenitentiae* (i.e., a period of time in which to repent) in order to seek restitution from the other party.

LOCUS SIGILLI (L.S.) (Contracts)

"The place of the seal." In early contract law, contracts were worthless unless the parties actually affixed a seal to the paper on which the contract itself was written. Like many formal contract requirements, the necessity of a seal gradually eroded (at least in the case of most ordinary contracts). One of the first steps in this process of erosion was the acceptance of the Latin phrase *Locus Sigilli* written on the document instead of the actual seal being affixed. Later the legal community began accepting abbreviation "L.S." in place of the Latin words.

LUCRI CAUSA (Criminal)

"For the sake of material gain." This term is used to describe the criminal intent involved when a person steals the property of another.

LUCRUM FACERE EX PUPILLI TUTELA TUTOR NON DEBET (Property)

"A guardian ought not reap a profit from the property of his/her ward." A guardian may exact a fee for managing an estate but s/he cannot use the ward's property for his/her (the guardian's) own gain.

■ M

MALA FIDES (General Terms)
"Bad faith."

MALUM IN SE (Criminal)
"Bad/evil in [and of] itself." Conduct that the law deems fundamentally (morally) wrong.

MALUM PROHIBITUM (Criminal)
"Bad/evil that is prohibited." Conduct that the law forbids. An act or omission that is *malum prohibitum* rather than *malum in se* lacks the morally distasteful connotation of the latter.

MANDAMUS * (Constitutional, Civil Procedure)

"We command." A party generally seeks a writ of *mandamus* when s/he believes that someone (typically a judge or administrative official) has abused his/her power by failing to perform a ministerial duty (i.e., a duty requiring no discretion) which s/he was legally bound to perform. The party asks the higher authority to say to the judge or administrative official, "We command you to perform your ministerial duty."

MENS REA * (Criminal)

"An evil mind." *Mens rea* is the mental component necessary to convict a person of a crime. It is the criminal intent, knowledge, recklessness, or negligence required as an element of any given crime.

MINUTIAE (General Terms)

"The very small things."

MOBILIA SEQUUNTUR PERSONAM (Property)

"Movable things follow the person." When an owner of movable property changes his/her domicile, the laws of the new domicile govern the movable property.

MODUS OPERANDI ("M-O") (General Terms)

"A manner of operating." Criminals often use a distinctive *modus operandi*. Prosecutors sometimes use the existence of a distinctive (sometimes said to be signature-like) *modus operandi* as a means of proving circumstantial evidence that a defendant who committed crime C must have been the same criminal who committed crimes A and B because crime C was committed in the same distinctive way—with the same signature-like *modus operandi*.

MODUS ET CONVENTIO VINCUNT LEGEM (Contracts)

"A course of dealing and agreement conquer law." In contract law parties may establish a custom of doing business or contract for performance with very few limits imposed by law.

MODUS VIVENDI (General Terms)

"A method of living." Lawyers often use the phrase *modus vivendi* to refer to a central principle in a field of law. For example, it is said that free competition is the *modus vivendi* of our American antitrust laws. In other words, our antitrust laws function because we believe that unrestrained competition is the most desired form of market economy.

MUTATIS MUTANDIS (General Terms)

"Since [some] things have changed [others] must change [also]." This phrase occurs in legal writing usually to indicate that because certain things have changed (e.g. the statute pursuant to which a court had based an earlier decision), others must necessarily change as a result of the change (e.g., a court's decision pursuant to the amended statute).

N

NE EXEAT REGNO (Civil Procedure)

"Let him/her not depart from the jurisdiction." This was the original name for a writ that forbids a person from leaving a county, state, country, etc. Parties seek such a writ when they fear that their adversary might attempt to leave without paying a sum due.

NEC VI, NEC CLAM, NEC PRECARIO* (Property)

"Neither by force, nor secretly, nor given as a favor." In order to acquire title to land by adverse possession, the adverse possessor cannot acquire the property by either forcefully taking it from its rightful owner, by taking it in secret, or by the owner giving the property to the adverse possessor freely.

NECESSITAS FACIT LICTUM QUOD ALIAS NON EST LICTUM (Criminal, Torts, General Terms)

"Necessity makes a thing lawful which on other occasions is not lawful."

NECESSITAS PUBLICA MAJOR EST QUAM PRIVATA (General Terms)

"Communal necessity is more important than the individual (necessity)."

NEMINE CONTRA DICENTE (General Terms)

"With no one speaking in opposition." When a court's opinion is unanimous, the decision can be characterized as *nomine contra dicente* (i.e., with no dissenting opinion).

NEMO BIS PUNITUR PRO EODEM DELICTO (Criminal, Constitutional)

"No one is punished twice for the same offense." The U.S. Constitution provides "nor shall any person be subject for the same offence to be twice put in jeopardy of life or limb." U.S. Const., amend. V.

NEMO BIS VEXARI PRO EADEM CAUSA (Criminal, Constitutional)
"No one [can be] troubled twice for the same reason." This maxim, like *Nemo bis punitur pro eodem delicto, supra,* expresses the concept that a defendant cannot be tried twice for the same crime (i.e., double jeopardy is not permitted in Anglo-American law).

NEMO DAT NON QUOD HABET (Contracts, Property)
"No one gives that which s/he does not have." A person can transfer to another only the interest in property which s/he him/herself owns. For example, someone who owns a life-estate cannot transfer a fee simple estate.

NEMO EST HERES VIVENTIS (Property, Wills, & Estates)
"No one is an heir of a living person." Technically, a person does not become an heir until the testator, testatrix, or intestate dies. In most jurisdictions, the word "heir" refers only to persons who will receive property from an intestate. Words like "legatee" or "devisee" are used for persons who will receive property under a will.

NEMO EST SUPRA LEGES (General Terms)
"No one is above the laws."

NEMO PLUS COMMODI HAEREDI SUO RELINQUIT QUAM IPSE HABUIT (Property, Wills & Estates)
"No one leaves behind more [of] bounty to his/her heir than s/he, himself/herself had." This maxim extends the principle, *nemo dat quod non habet, supra,* to the context of wills and estates.

NEMO PRAESUMITUR DONARE (Property)
"No one is assumed to make a present (to another)." This legal presumption helps to explain why the law of property generally requires certain specific elements as elements of valid gifts (e.g., donative intent, delivery, acceptance by the donee).

NEMO TENETUR SEIPSUM ACCUSARE
(Criminal, Constitutional)
"No one is held under sway to incriminate himself." The U.S. Constitution provides that "[n]o person... shall be compelled in any criminal case to be a witness against himself...." U.S. Const., amend. V.

NEXUS (Constitutional, General Terms)

"A binding, tying together, connecting." The word *nexus* is often used to indicate a necessary relationship in the law. It occurs in Constitutional law with respect to the concept of standing. In order to have standing to sue, a plaintiff must have a specific relationship that connects him/her to the controversy at issue.

NIHIL DICIT (Civil Procedure)

"S/he says nothing." When a defendant fails to plead (i.e., says nothing), the court grants a default judgment in favor of the plaintiff.

NIHIL HABET FORUM EX SCAENA (General Terms)

"A court of law considers nothing outside of the stage." The theatrical metaphor in the language of this maxim reflects the notion that the issues and litigants before a court are similar to a script and actors on stage. Simply stated, in American jurisprudence a court generally only decides issues that are properly before it.

NISI (General Terms)

"Unless." Courts often affix the word *nisi* to orders or rulings. In those instances, *nisi* indicates that the order or ruling will be final "unless" the losing (and even sometimes the prevailing) party moves to change that outcome (e.g., a trial judge's order might include the word *nisi* to indicate that the ruling will stand unless one of the parties appeals).

NISI PRIUS (General Terms)

"Unless before." *Nisi Prius* courts have traditionally been courts which have tried issues of fact to a jury. The judgments from these courts are final *unless* the losing party appeals *before* a certain date.

NOLENS VOLENS (General Terms)

"Unwilling [or] willing."

NOLLE PROSEQUI * (Criminal)

"To wish not to pursue." A prosecutor enters *nolle prosequi* (or "nolle" for short) on the record when s/he determines that a case is not worth the state's time, money, and/or effort to fully litigate.

NOLO CONTENDERE * (Criminal)

"I do not wish to contest." Unlike a person who pleads guilty, a person who pleads *nolo contendere* generally must have the court's permission to do so. A *nolo contendere* plea cannot be used against the person who pleads it in a subsequent civil case. Federal courts allow defendants to plead *nolo contendere* "only after due considera-tion of the view of the parties and the interest of the public in the effective administration of justice." *See* Fed. R. Crim. P. 11(c).

NON COMPOS MENTIS (Criminal)

"Not having control of the mind." A person who is *non compos mentis* generally cannot be criminally liable for his/her actions because s/he is incapable of possessing the requisite *mens rea.*

NON OBSTANTE VEREDICTO (Civil Procedure)

"With the verdict not standing in the way." After a jury has returned a verdict, if the losing party had previously requested a directed verdict, s/he may ask the court to grant a JNOV (judgment *non ob-stante verdicto*). If the judge, construing the evidence most favorably toward the party with the burden of persuasion, determines that reasonable people could not differ as to the result, s/he (the judge) may, in effect, reverse the jury by granting a JNOV.

NON SEQUITUR (General Terms)

"It does not follow." To assert that something is a *non sequitur* is to say that it does not logically follow from the preceding statement or argument.

NON SUB HOMINE SED SUB DEO ET LEGE (General Terms)

"Not under man but under God and law." This Latin maxim expresses the traditional Anglo-American ideal of the manner in which our so-ciety ought to conduct its affairs. Essentially, this phrase expresses the desire to keep a government of laws, not men.

NOSCITUR A SOCIIS (General Terms)

"It is known from its allies." This canon of statutory construction advises that unclear or ambiguous words in a statute (or contract) are best interpreted with reference to their context (i.e., by the *words* which are *allied* to the unclear or ambiguous word). Thus the "allies" (*sociis*) in this phrase are the words which comprise the context.

NOTA BENE (N.B.) (General Terms)

"Note well." Legal writers use this Latin phrase to call special at-tention to that which follows it. The abbreviation *N.B.* simply asks the reader to pay particular attention to what follows.

NUDUM PACTUM * (Contracts)

"A naked agreement." An agreement which is not supported by consideration.

NUNC PRO TUNC (General Terms)
"Now in place of then/Now fulfilling the place of then." Legal writers use this phrase to indicate the legal fiction that an event which occurred in the past is deemed to occur in the present.

■ O

OBITER DICTUM/DICTA (General Terms)
"A thing that has been said in passing." This is the complete phrase from which we get the simplified form, *dictum/dicta*. When a court merely comments about a situation, legal principle, or discusses how it might or would rule if the facts were different, legal writers characterize such statements by a court as *obiter dicta* (i.e., things that the court merely said incidentally—but not directly bearing on the outcome of the case at bar). *See also Dictum/Dicta, supra,* and *Ratio Decidendi, infra.*

OBLIGATIO (General Terms)
"The state of being legally liable."

OBLIGATIO EX CONTRACTU (Contracts)
"The state of being legally liable as a result of an agreement."

OBLIGATIO EX DELICTO (Torts)
"The state of being legally liable as a result of an offense."

OMNE MAJOR CONTINET IN SE MINUS (General Terms)
"Every larger thing contains in itself the lesser." This maxim, for example, applies to the principle in criminal law that a person charged with one offense can also be charged with the lesser offenses included within the primary charge.

OMNE TESTAMENTUM MORTE CONSUMATUM EST
(Property, Wills, & Estates)
"Every will is brought to maturity by death." A fundamental principle of the law of wills is that a will, by definition, has no legal effect until the testator/testatrix dies.

OMNIS INDEMNATUS PRO INNOXIS LEGIBUS HABETUR (Criminal)
"Everyone who has not been found guilty in a court of law is deemed innocent by the laws." In Anglo-American jurisprudence, the presumption that a person is innocent until proven guilty is a fundamental tenet.

ONUS PROBANDI (Civil Procedure, Criminal, General Terms)
"The burden of that which must be proved." A Latin phrase for "burden of proof."

OPTIMA EST LEGIS INTERPRES CONSUETUDO
(General Terms)
"The general practice of society/custom/convention is the most valid interpreter of law."

OPTIMUS INTERPRETANDI MODUS EST SIC LEGES INTERPRETARI UT LEGIBUS CONCORDANT (General Terms)
"The most valid method of interpreting laws is to construe them in such a way that they live in harmony with (other) laws." *See also In Pari Materia, supra.*

■ P

PACTA QUAE TURPEM CAUSAM CONTINENT NON SUNT OBSERVANDA (Contracts)
"Agreements that embrace a shameful/disgraceful/dishonorable/in-decent objective ought not be recognized." American contract law generally prohibits certain types of contracts because the subject matter is considered immoral or, at least, socially undesirable. For example, American antitrust laws are designed to make certain com-binations and price-fixing agreements illegal because they tend to stifle competition.

PACTA SUNT SERVANDA (Torts, Contracts)
"Agreements must be preserved." This Latin maxim expresses the traditional view that the agreements which the parties reach ought to be enforced to the greatest extent possible.

PAR * (Corporations & Tax)
"Equal, matching in magnitude or intensity." *Par* value stock today is less important than 50 or 100 years ago. Formerly, requirements of *par* value benefited stock purchasers and creditors because people could rely on a standard fixed value. Today many jurisdictions permit corporations to issue stock without *par* value.

PARENS PATRIAE (Constitutional)
"Parent of the native land." A state is said to be acting as *parens patriae* when a federal court grants the state standing to sue on behalf

of its residents. For example, in *Pennsylvania v. West Virginia*, 262 U.S. 553 (1924), the U.S. Supreme Court granted the state of Pennsylvania standing in order to protect the natural gas supply for both its public schools and individual consumers. The concept of *parens patriae* usually stretches the normal bounds of standing.

PARI PASSU (General Terms)
"In equal measure."

PARTICEPS CRIMINIS (Criminal)
"An accomplice of crime."

PASSIM (General Terms)
"Dispersedly; here and there; in every part." Legal writers use *passim* to indicate that support for the statement just made is not necessarily found in any one specific place (i.e., no one page or particular section) of the work cited. Rather, *passim* tells the reader that support for a statement occurs "here and there" in the cited article, book, etc.

PENUMBRA * (Constitutional)
"Almost shadow." The U.S. Supreme Court has held that the Bill of Rights casts penumbrae (e.g., the *penumbra* of privacy). The *penumbra* concept suggests that other individual rights, closely associated with those rights which the Bill of Rights grants, are implicitly protected (although not expressly included in the Bill of Rights itself).

PER CAPITA (Property, Wills & Estates, Tax)
"In accordance with the heads." Lawyers frequently use the phrase *per capita* in the field of tax, wills, and intestate succession. Taxes can be apportioned depending upon the number of individuals ("heads"). In the law of wills, an estate can be distributed to heirs or devisees in proportion to the number of heirs or devisees, without regard to the degree of kinship. Such a distribution is a *per capita* system of distribution.

PER CURIAM (General Terms)
"By the court." Most of the decisions which law students read in law school are written by one particular judge or justice. A *per curiam* opinion expresses the summary opinion of the concurring members of a court.

PER DIEM (Evidence & General Terms)
"By the day." The plaintiff's attorney in personal injury or wrongful death litigation generally likes to ask the jury to consider a *per diem*

argument for the apportionment of damages. For example, the lawyer would like to argue that the plaintiff or plaintiff's decedent is entitled to X number of dollars per day for enduring life with a particular handicap or enduring life without a spouse.

PER QUOD (Torts)
"Through which." This phrase is generally used when referring to libel *per quod*. When a libel is actionable *per quod*, the libelous statement itself is not actionable on its face; nevertheless the plaintiff alleges that s/he will show extrinsic facts *through which* it will become clear that the statement was, in fact, libelous.

PER SE * (General Terms, Torts)
"By itself." This phrase is often used in tort law to indicate that one set of circumstances creates a presumption that another thing exists. For example, if conduct is deemed negligence *per se* or slander *per se*, the plaintiff's burden of proof is substantially lower than it would have been otherwise. The court generally decides whether something is *per se* as a matter of law.

PER STIRPES (Property, Wills & Estates)
"By the families/ancestors from which one springs." *Per stirpes* is a system of succession whereby the decedent's estate is distributed on the basis of family relationship rather than the number of individual heirs.

PLENA AETAS (General Terms)
"Full/complete age."

POSSESSIO (Property)
"Possession/occupancy [of land or other property]." This term is materially different from the concept of ownership (*proprietas* or *dominum*).

POST HOC ERGO PROPTER HOC (General Terms)
"After this, therefore because of this." This phrase describes the logical fallacy that, because one event follows another chronologically, it was, therefore, caused by the first event. In short, simply because B follows A does not necessarily prove that A caused B.

POST LITEM MOTAM (Civil Procedure)
"After the lawsuit has been undertaken."

POST MORTEM (Criminal)

"After death." In murder cases a *post mortem* examination of the victim's body often reveals clues which may establish material facts (e.g., cause of death, time of death, what type of murder weapon was used, etc.).

PRAESUMPTIO JURIS (General Terms)

"A presumption of law."

PRETIUM (General Terms)

"Reward; punishment; price; something valuable; a fee; ransom."

PRIMA FACIE * (Evidence, Civil Procedure)

"By the first appearance." A plaintiff must prove a *prima facie* case in order to win a lawsuit. In order to prove a *prima facie* case, s/he must prove every essential element of his/her cause of action. For example, in order to prove a *prima facie* case of negligence, a plaintiff must prove: duty, breach, proximate/legal causation, and harm.

PRIMUS IN TEMPORE POTIOR EST IN JURE (Property)

"First in time is more powerful in law." A maxim of property law especially applicable in cases involving adverse possession or water rights. In certain circumstances, the first person to occupy or use property has a better legal claim to occupy or use that property than someone else who comes to or acquires the property later.

PRO BONO PUBLICO (General Terms)

"On behalf of the public good." When lawyers render services *gratis* (i.e., voluntarily without collecting fees), they generally do so *pro bono publico*. Most *pro bono* work is done on behalf of clients who could not otherwise afford legal services or who have causes which the lawyer deems sufficiently worthy in terms of social value.

PRO FORMA * (General Terms)

"According to form." Things done in a *pro forma* fashion typically are done appropriately with respect to overt, external procedural rules; however, they are likely to be substantively questionable or irresponsible. When something is done *pro forma*, it is done without examining the merits.

PRO HAC VICE (Civil Procedure)

"For this situation." In most jurisdictions it is possible for an attorney who is not admitted to practice law in that jurisdiction to be admitted in order to handle one particular lawsuit or legal matter. When a jurisdiction permits an attorney to practice law for one specific instance, the attorney is said to be admitted *pro hac vice*. Generally, an attorney files a motion with the court, requesting admission *pro hac vice*.

PRO RATA * (Corporations & Tax, Torts, Contracts)
"In relation to fixed proportions; according to that which has been reckoned." Corporations typically pay their shareholders dividends on a *pro rata* basis; that is, in proportion to the number of shares owned. Also, in quasi-contract actions, persons often recover damages based upon *pro rata* compensation for the time which s/he performed services for the defendant. See, e.g., *Britton v. Turner*, 6 N.H. 481 (1834).

PRO SE (Civil Procedure)
"On behalf of oneself." When a litigant acts as his/her own attorney, s/he is said to conduct the case *pro se*.

PRO TANTO
"For so much."

PRO TEMPORE (PRO TEM.) (General Terms)
"For the time [being]."

Q

QUANTUM MERUIT * (Contracts)
"How much s/he deserved." The measure of damages typically awarded in quasi-contract actions. This phrase expresses the notion that a person ought to recover according to the value of services performed.

QUANTUM VALEBAT (Contracts)
"How much it was worth." Like *quantum meruit, supra*, the phrase *quantum valebat* expresses a typical measure of damages in quasi-contract actions. A buyer is liable to a seller for the market value of goods delivered.

QUARE CLAUSUM FREGIT (Property, Torts)
"For what reason s/he violated the enclosed space." This was the technical title of the action that a landowner brought against an al-

leged trespasser in early common law. The *clausum* in this phrase refers to the landowner's physical space that the alleged trespasser violated.

QUASI (General Terms)
"As if."

QUASI EX CONTRACTU * (Contracts)
"As if out of contract." Also called quasi-contract. In many circumstances where, for one reason or another, no valid contract exists, a plaintiff may still sue a defendant in quasi-contract to recover the value of the benefit which s/he has bestowed upon the defendant.

QUASI IN REM (Civil Procedure)
"As if against the thing." Actions in which jurisdiction is *quasi in rem* are ostensibly actions against property but are, in reality, against a person. *Quasi in rem* type I suits are those suits in which a plaintiff's cause of action arises from the defendant's contacts with the forum. *Quasi in rem* type II suits are those suits in which a plaintiff's cause of action does not arise from the defendant's contacts with the forum.

**QUI TACET CONSENTIRE VIDETUR, UBI TRACTATUR
DE EJUS COMMODO*** (Evidence)
"S/he who says nothing appears to agree deliberately, when that which is being discussed concerns his/her interest." This maxim expresses the belief that a person can admit facts and other things by silence. The *Miranda* decision and other personal rights limit the use of silence as an admission of guilt but the maxim still has some utility in the law of evidence.

QUI TAM (Civil Procedure)
"Who so as." A *qui tam* action is a civil suit brought by a person who acts, in part, on behalf of the state. For example, the federal unfair housing laws permit plaintiffs who have knowledge of certain violations to sue those who have violated unfair housing statutes. If successful, *qui tam* plaintiffs keep a statutory share of the recovery from the defendant and the state gets a share as well.

QUIA EMPTORES (Property)
"Because the buyers." This is the name of the statute passed in England in 1290 that provided that all future alienations of land would be deemed to occur by substitution rather than by subinfeudation.

QUID PRO QUO * (Contracts, General Terms)
"What for what." A phrase which describes the things which parties to a contract exchange. The *quid pro quo* is the Latin term for the consideration which supports a contract.

QUORUM * (Corporations, General Terms)
"Of whom." The minimum number of group members necessary for that group to make valid and binding decisions.

▮ R

RATIO DECIDENDI * (General Terms)
"Rationale of reaching a decision." The reasoning which explains the principle of law articulated in a case. The court's explanation of the holding.

RATIONE SOLI * (Property)
"By reason of the land." A concept in property law by which *ferae naturae* (wild animals) belong to the person who owns the land upon which they (the animals) live. Most jurisdictions presume that in-animate objects also belong to a property owner by *ratione soli*.

REDUCTIO AD ABSURDUM (General Terms)
"A leading-back to absurdity." A phrase from the discipline of logic indicating that an argument is so structured as to lead to a logically inconsistent or absurd result.

REMITTITUR (Civil Procedure)
"It is sent back." When a judge or court determines that a jury has awarded a plaintiff too much money, the judge or court may order a *remittitur* (i.e., that the plaintiff return a portion of the award to the defendant).

RES COMMUNIS (Property)
"A thing belonging to, concerning, or shared by each of two persons." Certain states (e.g., California) are community property states. In those states, the legal presumption exists that all property acquired by both a husband and wife during the tenure of marriage belongs to both spouses as joint owners. Each item of property is a *res communis*.

RES GESTAE * (Evidence)

"Things that have been done." Courts have used this term to refer to certain types of statements that are either exceptions to hearsay or not hearsay at all. The phrase *res gestae* today is mostly of historical interest. Modern rules of evidence characterize the types of statements that used to be called *res gestae* as present sense impressions, statements concerning the declarant's physical condition, excited utterances, or statements regarding present mental or emotional state.

RES INTER ACTOS ALIA, ALIIS NEQUE NOCERE NEQUE PRODESSEE POTEST (Civil Procedure)

"A thing done between some is neither able to injure nor benefit others." This maxim expresses the central precept of *res judicata, infra.*

RES IPSA LOQUITUR * (Torts)

"The thing, itself, speaks." When a plaintiff can prove: (a) that his/her injury does not ordinarily occur without someone's negligence; (b) that the instrumentality which caused the injury was or should have been in the complete control of the defendant; and (c) that s/he (the plaintiff) was not negligent; then the plaintiff has proven a *prima facie* case under the theory of *res ipsa loquitur.* The plaintiff need not prove the ordinary elements of negligence.

RES JUDICATA * (Civil Procedure)

"A thing which has been decided." When one competent court has already ruled on a specific issue or claim, another court (other than an appropriate appeals court) cannot decide the same claim or issue a second time if: (1) the issue or claim in the prior adjudication was identical with the one presented in the action in question; (2) the first court issued a final judgment on the merits; and (3) the party against whom the plea is asserted is a party or in privity with a party to the prior adjudication.

RES NULLIUS (Property)

"A thing of no one." This term refers to things which have never before been owned by anyone (e.g., wild animals, fish, jewels which have never before been excavated). The ancient Roman concept, *occupatio*, provides that a person acquires ownership of a *res nullius* by taking possession of it and by intending to retain possession of it.

RESPONDEAT SUPERIOR * (Torts)

"Let the one above reply." The tort law doctrine which holds an employer responsible for the torts committed by its employee, when the employee was acting within the scope of his/her employment.

S

SCIENTER (Criminal Law, Torts)

"Knowingly, consciously." Most crimes and many civil wrongs entail a mental element. In many circumstances the law will require that a person have knowledge of certain facts before legal sanctions follow. Statutes and common law formulations often refer to the knowledge requirement as *scienter*. For example, we might say that the defendant did not have *scienter*, therefore s/he is not liable.

SCINTILLA (Evidence)

"A particle of fire, spark." Judges and lawyers occasionally say that there is not a *scintilla* of evidence to show something. In other words, not even a tiny spark to shed light on the issue.

SCIRE FACIAS (Civil Procedure)

"May you bring [it] about to know." This is the name of a writ at common law that directs the person to whom it is directed to explain (i.e., "cause to know") why the moving party should not prevail. For example, if A had won a contract suit against B and the court had awarded money damages, A could bring a writ of *scire facias* to require B to explain why s/he (A) should not have the money awarded in the original action.

SIC UTERE TUO UT ALIENUM NON LAEDAS * (Property, Torts)

"Use your own [property] in such a way that you do not harm another." A maxim of property law which holds that a person is free to use his/her property in any way s/he sees fit so long as s/he does not harm others (or the property of others). This phrase often occurs in connection with the concept of nuisance.

SINE DIE (General Terms)

"Without a day." This phrase is used when courts or legislative bodies adjourn their proceedings without designating a specific time to reconvene (i.e., "without a day" designated to meet again).

SINE PROLE (Property, Wills & Estates)
"Without issue." When a person dies without having had any children (and without any children having been conceived prior to death), the decedent is said to have died *sine prole*.

SINE QUA NON (General Terms)
"Not without which." Legal writers often use this phrase to denote the crucial component part without which a whole would not exist. One might say, for example, that consideration is the *sine qua non* of every enforceable contract.

SITUS (Property, Contracts, General Terms)
"The particular position occupied by a thing." Lawyers often refer to the *situs* of property or the *situs* of a contract. Often the principles of conflict of laws must determine the *situs* of property or agreements.

STARE DECISIS * (et non quieta movere) (Civil Procedure)
"To stand firmly by things that have been decided (and not to rouse/ disturb/move things at rest)." This is the complete maxim from which the shortened phrase *stare decisis* comes. Under this principle of common law, courts resolve the cases presently before them in the same way that cases with similar facts have been resolved in the past.

STATUS QUO (General Terms)
"Standing at which." A phrase found in law to explain that matters will remain as before.

SUA SPONTE * (General Terms)
"Of one's own volition, of his/her/its/their own volition, voluntarily." For example, courts often decide to review the question of jurisdiction *sua sponte*, without a party raising the issue.

SUB JUDICE (General Terms)
"Under the authority of a judge." Lawyers use the phrase *sub judice* to refer to the case that they are currently litigating. Lawyers often use it when explaining why their case is either similar to or different from another case (e.g., "Your honor, case X had a plaintiff who had done X, Y, Z, but in the case *sub judice*, (i.e., the case presently before you) the plaintiff did A, B, and C").

SUB NOMINE (General Terms)
"Under the name." Occasionally the name of a case changes as the parties' positions in litigation change (e.g., *Smith v. Jones* will be-

come *Jones v. Smith* on appeal if Smith wins at the trial court level). Case names can also change for other reasons. For example a case titled *X, Y, Z Corp. v. A, B, C Corp.* can change to *L, M, N, O, P Corp. v. A, B, C. Corp.* if L, M, N, O, P Corp. merges with or acquires X, Y, Z Corp. during the litigation. When a case's name changes, a judge, attorney, or commentator may refer to the case as having previously had another name. For example, in our *X, Y, Z Corp. v. A, B, C Corp.* hypothetical, after the case name had changed to *L, M, N, O, P Corp. v. A, B, C Corp.*, a writer might comment that the judge had ruled on the motion for summary judgment *sub nomine X, Y, Z Corp. v. A, B, C Corp.*

SUB SILENTIO (General Terms)
"Under shelter of silence." A thing is done *sub silentio* when it is done without expressly indicating that it has been done. For example, a court might overrule a previous case *sub silentio* (i.e. without expressly stating that it was overruling the precedent).

SUBPOENA (Criminal)
"Under penalty." A *subpoena* is a document which commands a person to appear (usually to testify as a witness) at trial. If a person who has been subpoenaed does not comply with the terms of the subpoena, s/he is subject to sanctions by the court.

SUBPOENA DUCES TECUM * (Civil Procedure)
"Under penalty, you will bring with you." A *subpoena duces tecum* commands the person to whom it is directed to produce books, papers, documents, or other tangible things.

SUI GENERIS * (General Terms)
"Of its own kind." Cases with unusual or unique facts ("one of a kind" in our idiom) are said to be *sui generis*.

SUPERSEDEAS (Civil Procedure)
"You may sit [in an official capacity] above." When a court grants a stay of proceedings or a stay of execution of an order, the writ is often referred to as a *supersedeas* writ. In essence, one writ supersedes the other.

SUPRA (General Terms)
"Above." Legal writers use the word *supra* to indicate that the reference to which they just alluded appears "above" or earlier in their text.

■ T

TESTAMENTUM OMNE MORTE CONSUMMATUR
(Property, Wills & Estates)
"A will is reckoned up/brought to maturity entirely by death." In modern estates practice lawyers say that "a will speaks from the time of death." This idea is relatively simple. Because of its very nature, a will has no legal effect regarding the disposition of a person's property until the person who made the will dies.

TESTATOR/TESTATRIX (Property, Wills & Estates)
"One who makes a will." From the Latin verb *testari*, "to bear witness to, to declare, to call to witness." Since property law necessarily involves the study of property transfers, law students often meet the terms *testator* (male) and *testatrix* (female) in their study of gifts.

TESTES PONDERANTUR, NON NUMERANTUR (Evidence)
"Witnesses are weighed, not counted." Judges often remind the members of the jury that the number of witnesses produced by one side or the other should not shape their opinion. Rather, juries should carefully consider what each witness has said and assess each witness's credibility.

■ U

UBI JUS IBI REMEDIUM (General Terms & Torts)
"Where (there is) a right there is a remedy." This Latin maxim expresses the notion that if a person possesses a right, the violation of that right by another necessarily gives rise to a legal or equitable remedy.

ULTRA VIRES * (Corporations, General Terms)
"Beyond the powers." Before modern corporate statutes expanded the legal capacity of corporations, courts limited the powers of corporations only to those powers specifically delineated in the articles of incorporation. When a corporation attempted to do something that the articles of incorporation had not specifically provided for, courts held that such an act was *ultra vires*. Today the Model Business Corporation Act has narrowed the applicability of the doctrine. *See* MBCA 3.04.

UXOR (UX.) (General Terms)
"Wife."

■ V

VEL NON (General Terms)
"Whether or not." *Vel non* is found in legal writing merely as short-hand for "whether or not."

VENIRE FACIAS (Civil Procedure, General Terms)
"You may cause to come." These are the first words of a common law writ instructing a sheriff "to cause" jurors "to come" for trial.

VI ET ARMIS (Torts, Property, General Terms)
"With force and tools/implements/arms." In old cases for trespass, a plaintiff often alleged that the defendant had damaged the property by using force or some device (i.e., *vi et armis*).

VIS MAJOR (Contracts)
"A greater force." Many contracts state that certain occurrences which are beyond the control of the parties (e.g., acts of God, acts of war, fire, flood, etc.) do not impose liability on the party damaged thereby. Such an occurrence is often referred to as a *vis major*.

VIVA VOCE (Evidence)
"With a living voice." Evidence that is given by live testimony (i.e., a person who appears and testifies in court) is generally preferred to evidence in affidavits or other documents. Lawyers say that oral testimony is given *viva voce*.

VOLENTI NON FIT INJURIA* (Torts)
"To one who is willing there is no injury." This Latin phrase ex-presses the tort doctrine of assumption of risk. For example, a ra-cecar driver will probably lose a suit against another driver on the track whose negligence caused him/her injury, because s/he has vol-untarily assumed the risk of such injury (even when caused by the negligence of another driver).

PRONUNCIATION GUIDE*

■ VOWELS

The following rules are invariable.

Short Vowels		Long Vowels	
a as in cart	charta	ā as in *father*	fabula
e as in *bed*	est, sed	ē as in *they*	se, desiderat
i as in *pin*	timida	ī as in *machine*	insula
o as in *domain*	novus	ō as in *note*	non
u as in *put*	nunc	ū as in *rude*	luna
	y¹ as in French *tu*	cygnus	

■ DIPHTHONGS

ae as in *aisle*	terrae	eu e+u in one syllable	Europa
oe as in *oil*	Phoenicia	ui u+i in one syllable	cui
au as in *out*	laudat	ei as in *vein*	deinde

* Reprinted from *Latin Via Ovid* by Norma Goldman and Jacob E. Nyenhuis, by permission of the Wayne State University Press. Copyright © 1977 by Wayne State University Press. Second Edition © 1982 by Wayne State University Press, Detroit, Michigan 48202. All rights reserved.

■ CONSONANTS

Latin and English consonants are pronounced alike with the following reservations:

c	is always hard as in *can*	**Cicero**
g	is always hard as in *give*	**argentum**
i	can be a consonant, sounded as *y* in *year* when it occurs in a consonant position[2]	**Iuppiter, iam, iustus, huius**
r	is tongue-trilled	**vocare, sonare**
s	is always hissed as a voiceless consonant, *sea*, never voiced as *z* in was	**soror, insula, casa**
t	is always sounded *t* as in *tin*, never *sh* as in *oration*	**teneo, initio**
v	has the sound of *w*	**parva, voco**
x	has the sound of *ks*	**exemplum**
bs, bt	are sounded *ps* and *pt*	**urbs, obtineo**
ch	is related to Greek *chi* and is close to *kh* in *blockhouse*	**chorus**
ph	is related to Greek *phi* and is close to *ph* in *uphill*	**amphora**
th	is related to Greek *theta* and is close to *th* in *pothook*	**theatrum**

Double consonants: **ss, tt, ll**, etc., are sounded twice the length of time given to the single consonant.

■ SYLLABLES

A Latin word has as many syllables as it has vowels or diphthongs. The vowel alone or the consonant and vowel together can make the syllable. Divide words according to the following rules:

1. A consonant is pronounced with the vowel that follows it: **a.ma.mus**.
2. When two vowels (or a vowel and a diphthong) occur together, pronounce them separately: **fi.li.a, e.os, vi.ae**.
3. When two consonants occur together, pronounce them separately: **por.to pu.el.la, ma.gis.ter**. A stop consonant (b, p, d, t, c, g) followed by a liquid (l or r) counts as a single consonant: **ma.tris, fra.tris, ne.glec.tus**.
4. When more than two consonants occur together, the first generally is pronounced with the preceding vowel and the others with the following: **mon.strum, cas.tra, ex.em.plum**.
5. Separate compound words into the original parts: **trans.porto, ab.rogo, ex.animo, com.es, in.eo sub.ire**.

■ LONG AND SHORT SYLLABLES

1. A syllable is long if it contains a long vowel or a diphthong. Such a syllable is said to be long by nature: **in.su.la, fa.bu.la, Phoe.ni.ci.a, a.moe.na.**
2. A syllable is long if it contains a short vowel followed by two consonants (except a stop followed by a liquid).[3] Such a syllable is said to be long by position: **ma.gis.ter, Mi.ner.va.**
3. All other syllables are short.

■ ACCENT

1. In words of two syllables, accent the first syllable (the penult).

   á.mant   pú.er   cár.ta   nó.vus

   The last syllable is called the *ultima*, from the Latin **ultimus**, meaning "last." The next to the last syllable is called the *penult*, from the Latin **paene**, meaning "almost" and **ultimus**. The syllable before the *penult* is called the *antepenult*, from the words **ante**, meaning "before," and *penult*.
2. In words of more than two syllables, accent the penult *if it is long*: **habitare, docere, amoenas, magister.** It may be long by nature or by position. Otherwise accent the antepenult: **insula, fabula, filia.** This rule for determining accent is called the *antepenultimate rule*, and it never varies.

Examples:

	Antepenult	*Penult*	*Ultima*
portare	por	**ta**	re
regina	re	**gi**	na
spectate	spec	**ta**	te
amoena	a	**moe**	na
taurus		**tau**	rus
terra		**ter**	ra
puella	pu	**el**	la
magister	ma	**gis**	ter
fabula	**fa**	bu	la
insula	**in**	su	la
filia	**fi**	li	a
incola	**in**	co	la
agricola	a	**gri**	co	la

On what basis do present-day grammarians state the rules for the pronunciation of a language which was never verbally recorded and which is pronounced so differently in various parts of the world? Certainly, Latin pronounced by an

Englishman and by a German and by an Italian (and by the Church which historically grew within the Italian framework of pronunciation) is quite different from that which we teach as Classical Latin. The sources for our reconstruction of how Latin must have sounded in classical times are many: first, the direct evidence in the writings of ancient grammarians; second, poetry properly scanned to indicate the length of vowels; third, ancient puns and approximations of animal cries; fourth, the spellings on inscriptions; fifth, the spellings in Latin for words borrowed from other languages and the spellings in other languages for Latin words (e.g., **kaisar** in Greek assures us that the **c** was hard); sixth, the pronunciation of the dialects of Latin and of Vulgar Latin; and last, comparative grammar.[4] On these bases, scientific scholarship has reconstructed a pronunciation of Latin which was adopted decades ago in the United States and which tries to reproduce the way Latin was spoken in Classical Rome, c. 200 B.C. to c. 200 A.D.

■ ENDNOTES

1. Both long and short; especially used in borrowed words of Greek origin. Also sounded as Latin u to approximate the Greek upsilon.

2. Either at the beginning of a word followed by a vowel, or between two vowels.

3. The second of these consonants begins the following syllable (**in.su.la**). A syllable containing a short vowel followed by a stop and a liquid may be either long or short.

4. Roland G. Kent, *The Sounds of Latin* (Baltimore: Waverly Press, 1940), pp. 31, 43.